Praise for *I Love You. Now What?*

"Mabel continues to show us the practical applications of loving and being loved without breaking the magical enchantment of love."
— Lissette Valdés-Valle, journalist

"It's without a doubt the best guide I have ever read for real, intimate and long-lasting relationships. Whether you're married, single, with or without love interest, this book is a must."
— Julia Dangond, senior TV and entertainment executive

"Mabel Iam offers a practical guide for keeping love alive and finding, once and for all, a perfect and harmonious relationship."
— Julio César Paredes, *El Diario/La Prensa*

"I've been really moved. This book is full of tenderness worth enjoying."
— José Antonio Ponseti, programming director, Caracol Radio

I Love You.
Now What?

I Love You.
Now What?

*Falling in Love Is a Mystery,
Keeping It Isn't*

MABEL IAM

ATRIA BOOKS
New York   London   Toronto   Sydney

ATRIA BOOKS

A Division of Simon & Schuster, Inc.
1230 Avenue of the Americas
New York, NY 10020

Copyright © 2008 by Corpo Solar, Inc.

All rights reserved, including the right to reproduce this book or portions thereof in any form whatsoever. For information address Atria Books Subsidiary Rights Department, 1230 Avenue of the Americas, New York, NY 10020

First Atria Books trade paperback edition January 2008

ATRIA BOOKS and colophon are trademarks of Simon & Schuster, Inc.

For information about special discounts for bulk purchases,
please contact Simon & Schuster Special Sales at 1-800-456-6798
or business@simonandschuster.com.

Designed by Kyoko Watanabe

Manufactured in the United States of America

10   9   8   7   6   5   4   3   2   1

Library of Congress Cataloging-in-Publication Data
Iam, Mabel.
    I love you, now what? : falling in love is a mystery, keeping it isn't / by Mabel Iam.—1st Atria Books trade pbk. ed.
        p. cm.
1. Man-woman relationships. 2. Love. 3. Couples. I. Title.

HQ801.I23 2008
646.7'8—dc22
                                                                    2007011240

ISBN-13: 978-1-4165-3995-7
ISBN-10:   1-4165-3995-6

I dedicate this book to the love of my life, my husband, Greg.

Our love story, like many others, is very romantic. Even though we lived six thousand miles apart, we fell in love in 2000. When we declared our love for one another, I remember both of us saying, "I love you. Now what?"

Today, a number of years later, I can proudly affirm that we still feel the same way for each other, and that this feeling grows daily without boundaries, embellished with happiness, passion, harmony and light. Thank you, my love.

Contents

❧

PART TWO

Sexuality: Now What?

Preface

⁂

Readers and journalists most often ask me: Mabel, do you really believe love can be perfect?

I am convinced that love is perfect and that some relationships can be totally radiant. I believe that when you feel love, the differences between partners help you grow as human beings. Issues can be worked out in relationships just as diamonds can be cut and polished to a perfect brilliance. Although I have devoted my life to writing books about relationships and love, most of my readers don't know the real reason why.

Throughout my life, the person who most influenced my thoughts, actions, beliefs and feelings was my maternal grandmother. Her name was Maria and she lived through an amazing love story. It was a very special story of love, fidelity and hope. It seems like an unforgettable novel but is actually a true account of her life. I never told this story in a book before. I guess I never considered it important to reveal my personal motivations. But as I was writing this book, the memory of my grandmother's story and her presence in my heart felt very intense. It seemed as if she was with me, blessing me, and I often saw her in my dreams while writing one of my most cherished books—the very book that you are holding right now.

My grandparents were born in Ukraine, which at that time was part of the Russian Empire and ruled by czars. My grandparents, like many European emigrants, believed in the promise of the Americas; as young newlyweds they packed up their dreams and migrated to Argentina.

When my grandmother was around twenty-one, she returned to Ukraine to visit her parents, along with her two small sons, who later became my uncles. At that time, of course, there were no airplanes, computers, fax machines, e-mails or any of that. People traveled the world by ship. My grandfather was working in Argentina, where they had a house, so he stayed behind waiting for his wife to return. But something terrible happened while she was away: World War I erupted and Russia experienced a revolution that the whole world is familiar with. My grandmother was not able to return to Argentina for seven years. She was unable to communicate with my grandfather, because international communication was a nightmare in those days, prohibited by restrictions imposed by the Russian government. My grandmother told me many times that during the revolution she suffered horrific events and moments of absolute terror.

After seven years abroad, she was finally able to return to Argentina with her two children in tow. Amazingly, as if life were a fairy tale, she found my grandfather—still waiting for her just as he had been the day she left. He hadn't started a new life or become involved with another woman, even though he hadn't heard a word from her in all those years. My grandfather might have imagined that his wife and children had died, or that she might have perhaps married another man. He could have imagined any number of things and elected to start a new life, but he didn't. He had faith in his love above all else. Once reunited, they produced two more children, the younger of which was the beautiful and enigmatic Florinda, who later became my mother.

This is really a story of limitless fidelity and love: a love that survived time, distance and war.

Having grown up with this fascinating anecdote in my life, I believe that my mission is to help love transcend every limit, explore every possibility and come out triumphant and perfect, like the love between my grandparents Maria and Adolfo.

—*Mabel Iam*

Acknowledgments

I would like to thank:

My spiritual teacher Meishu Sama, who inspires my days with his eternal light.

My beloved and irreplaceable friend Johanna, who believed in me and my work. I thank her from the bottom of my heart for granting me the opportunity to be the godmother of her child, one of the most marvelous and unique gifts I have ever received. I am honored and proud to be in her life.

My dear Alfonso, my sweet godchild who has offered me great happiness and light in my life.

My parents and grandparents, who guide me from the heavens with their love.

My brother Rafael, who offers me, with his generosity and love, the opportunity to enjoy my nieces and nephew who light up my life.

My beloved nieces and nephew: Ezequiel, my sweet, affectionate and divine godson; Manuela, my tender, feminine friend; and Caterina, a beam of sunshine filled with joy and creativity.

My husband's children, to whom I am honored to extend myself as a second mother: my good friend Gregory, the handsome Chris and his beautiful wife, Kristy.

Judith, who directs Atria with her elevated consciousness of light and love: may you be blessed for the faith that you have demonstrated in my work.

Amy, who always helps me with a sweet smile on her face.

My cousins Adolfo and Diana, who carry the memory of my maternal lineage, and who influenced my childhood with beauty and creativity.

My exquisite friend Dinorah, who helped me to shed light upon my words.

Maria, the angel who helps me out at home with so much love.

Peter, a loyal friend to both my husband and me.

My dear friend Ted, who is always there when either my husband or I need him.

Maumi and Ray, my sweet friends.

My beloved readers, for being so loyal and supportive. You represent the inspiration, the blessing, the love, the beginning and the end of every word that I write. I wish you much love and many blessings.

Introduction

Love is beyond reason. Love is not measurable in words.

Love cannot be partial; it cannot have owners. Love is essentially beyond definition or concept.

We have spent days, years and centuries seeking the keys to open our own locks, the doors that we have used to shut out our own happiness. And we don't realize that the only thing we have to do is open our hearts to love.

—MABEL IAM

One day we meet. Both of us feel an attraction, we kiss, we grow fond of one another, we make love and grow more fond, and then more so until we fall in love. But . . . now what? What happens after that?

At the beginning we are infatuated, and it is often difficult for us to keep our attention focused on our work or any other pastime; we think about him or her all day long. Although we become infatuated for very different and specific reasons, all human beings vibrate similarly. When we meet that special person, we're captivated by characteristics that we like and are attracted to: their mannerisms or behavior, the way they move, their beauty, or their intelligence. In fact, sometimes we cannot even find a single objective reason to justify our feelings.

Extraordinary things happen to us when we fall in love. We want to spend as much time as possible with our beloved. We assume that this person possesses extraordinary qualities, that he or she is the best human being on earth.

The person we are idealizing probably doesn't deserve to be boxed into one extreme category or another—neither a sum of virtues nor a tally of flaws—but the frustration that we experience upon realizing our biased perceptions can cause us to feel depressed and lead us to the most extravagant and exaggerated conclusions. Once this occurs, frustration takes over and smashes the mirror into which we have projected our needs and, especially, our dependence.

From the very first date, we feel uncertainty, fear, excitement, commitment, disappointment, suffering, illness, passion, the desire to escape and be alone again, love and confusion. All of these feelings and emotions get jumbled together, until we ask ourselves "Now what?" or "Why?" or "How will this movie turn out?" After all, our own story is far more interesting than any soap opera on TV.

Sometimes the tender love story turns into a drama or even a horror film. Unlike fiction, this nightmare has no ending. Often it continues until the relationship deteriorates entirely. The players end up exhausted and disillusioned. They may feel sensations such as cold, heat, heart palpitations and trembling. Everything experienced in that moment is lived with the greatest intensity, but also with tremendous insecurity. Our emotions range from absolute joy to deep sorrow and even fear of abandonment. Each of us is different, and, since each of us creates our own relationships, every situation is unique. Nonetheless, the way in which each of us creates or experiences relationships is significantly similar among all humans.

Problems and conflicts begin to repeat themselves, and we have no idea how to avoid them. This is when we decide to end the relationship to prevent suffering and avoid feeling pain.

Perhaps, out of fear of being alone, we enter into another relationship; perhaps not. After a while we begin to make the same mistakes with a new person. Even if we move to a different country, leave the planet, change our sex or switch religions, we haven't learned the answer to the following questions:

- How does one create a relationship so deep that it will not be eroded by obstacles?
- How does one generate a relationship that is sincere, clean, clear and real?
- Why do some of us associate love with drama?
- How can we allow the relationship to grow beyond life's ups and downs?
- Are human beings programmed for conflict?
- Why do we have certain feelings if they can be so destructive and cause so many problems?
- Do we know how to relate to love?

What Actually Happens in Relationships?

Relationships have been complex throughout history. Is there some type of fatal programming within us that works against love?

Everybody wants love, in all its forms—physical or sentimental—even if it's just the detached tenderness of choosing someone to test out a relationship for a moment, a short-term basis or perhaps for the rest of their lives.

In spite of advances in the field of psychology, sophisticated scientific technologies designed to study the human mind and body, a higher standard of living, and all the information available on how to improve relationships, we are still in the dark.

The thousands of questions I receive on my website—in different languages, from different countries and cultures—seem as if they come from the same person. The themes of lost love, jealousy, abandonment, anguish and anxiety continually repeat themselves. Pain, grief and deception intoxicate love's metabolism, and sadly, much as they do in the body, these toxic emotions accumulate in the soul.

This book doesn't contain all the answers to human conflict. The difference between this and other books is its approach to the problem and its solutions. The more we understand the causes and motives behind any conflict, the easier it is to resolve it.

Now What?

Every outcome in life is caused by something that, consciously or not, we are responsible for. In our relationships, it is very easy to project our own limitations, frustrations, desires or fantasies onto our partner. These mechanisms sooner or later generate conflicts, especially when we do not accept our responsibility for choosing our relationships.

The Three Golden Steps to Great Relationships

Before you can create a successful and harmonious partnership, you must keep the following in mind:

- Understand why you desire a mate.
- Know and be conscious of what you want to achieve in creating a union.
- Once you know what you want in a relationship and know it as clearly in your mind as in your heart, you can choose the right person by taking advantage of the best possible moment, one in which you feel truly open.

About This Book

The most important objective of this book is to help you learn about your inner self to improve your relationships by making them more loving each day.

This book is divided into two parts. The first part, "Love: Now

What?" reflects upon questions such as: What do I do with this love? Why do I love him or her? Why doesn't this person love me? Why am I attracted to this person? Why does he or she reject me? Along with all the thousands of questions that invade our minds, we'll also analyze how, after an intimate encounter, the opposite seems to unfold—lack of intimacy and affection, sexual miscommunication and the like. In what manner do these circumstances negatively affect us and the relationship? This section also includes personal testimonials for us to better understand why different conflicts occur between people who love one another.

The second part, "Sexuality: Now What?", contains techniques for improving sexual communication as well as increasing awareness of our own body and emotions. All of the exercises in the book are designed to improve your romantic relationships and, by extension, your life.

Love is the foundation upon which our entire world is created. All of our interactions emerge from the same principle of love. Without love, it would be impossible to live. Even in spite of the doubts that continue to cloud our minds, as you read these pages, trust in love. Now, let's get to the task of working to master it.

Part One

LOVE: NOW WHAT?

To fascinate the other with a glance, sighing with desire for a kiss.

To storm through the heart's ice with fire.

To caress the dream of an encounter.

To toast with effervescent lust.

To suspend our breath until we breathe in excitement.

Life is a continuous lure and invitation to love.

Would you like to come in or stay outside and miss the party?

CHAPTER 1

I Love You and I Love Myself

Do I have any idea what kind of relationship I need?

Am I prepared for true love?

Have I dreamed of the possibility of finding a perfectly harmonious relationship?

Do I dare to live out this dream?

Do I know my personality, what I can and cannot give, and that which I need to receive in order for the relationship to work?

While asking myself these questions, I can learn the answers that flow straight from my heart.

The Mystery of Love

No other human activity is initiated with such powerful hopes and expectations as an amorous relationship. This is true even for those who have failed or encountered obstacles with other relationships. At the start of a new relationship, the enthusiasm of gambling on love is always renewed. And, unlike most of life's activities, falling in love is not something we can plan ahead of time. It just happens.

It also happens sometimes without our realizing it. We may find ourselves involved in a relationship and asking ourselves, "How did

I get here?" Then we realize that the words *I love you* have escaped our hearts and our lips. Then we ask, "What now?"

Every human being goes through this, in some way at some point. It's that marvelous aspect of love and relationships that cannot be controlled as other activities can. And this is why so many questions arise after we hear ourselves affirm our love.

Love is the path that guides us to a life of abundance and perfection. This is the first thing we need to understand about love, which leads us to the fact that a relationship is always in a state of renewal, even when we are relating to ourselves. It is important that we reflect daily that when we are in a relationship we must always remain open to newness.

A romantic relationship is a continuous exchange of emotions, ideas, opinions, wills, beliefs, actions, reactions, vibrations, thoughts and objectives between two people. The foundation for happiness is set when this exchange is positive and balanced. Through it, love can be rediscovered and shared by way of trust, understanding, gentleness, union and acceptance.

Should There Be a School for Love?

I have always said that nobody has educated us on how to love. Religions across the ages, without a doubt, have had some say in the matter, yet conflicts, divorces and problems seem to increase more and more each day.

Questions about love are endless: Can one learn to love? Are we capable of loving more than one person? How many relationships should we have before deciding which will be "the one"? Can we really love someone all of our lives? Are there universal ideas regarding love or does everything depend upon the culture in which we were raised? Do we generally only place value on learning things that can bring us money or prestige? How many times have we mistaken passion for love? I could go on and on asking questions. This book could become a dictionary of questions. Let us each begin to think about creating a school for love that will unify all human beings from anywhere on the planet.

Among the many answers I have found, I believe that love is the most beautiful and simple art in life. Love, as any art, is learned. In fact, the desire to efficiently and consciously solidify a relationship is an act of maturity. This process, when carried out by both members of the relationship, is splendid and very gratifying for the couple on the material, emotional, mental and spiritual levels. If we wish to learn how to love, we must proceed in the same way we would to master anything else.

Love benefits every level of our existence. It nurtures and sustains every act and situation that we go through in our lives. Thanks to this, it is life's central theme and the primary area on which we have to focus our energies. Yes, whether we want to admit it or not, all of us will fall in love at some point in our lives. We may feel lost while navigating this wondrous art because for this, the most interesting of all human activities, there is no school.

Every relationship that we undertake in life helps us grow, be it through painful or pleasant experiences. Not all relationships work out, but all pass through our lives for some special purpose. Every time we need to learn something, we attract people who will help us find the answers. Only that one specific experience or that one particular relationship holds the key to teaching us the true answer.

Our relationships act as a mirror of our inner selves. That is why we have to take the following motto into account: "That which I love in others is me. That which I reject in others is also me."

We have the power to accept, modify and grow from any virtue or defect we encounter in ourselves. We can also carry out this same process in relationships, to deepen our love and trust for both ourselves and our significant other.

That which bonds us to another person is based on thoughts, beliefs, judgments and emotions. If we have a negative experience with someone and don't forgive him or her, we relate negatively to that person and remain negatively bound to our own emotions and thoughts. Later we may find that we end up repeating the same experience with somebody else.

If we remember the example of the mirror, we can change our view of the world and our own relationships. We can apply the law of attraction to find that special person who will correspond perfectly with our own feelings and thoughts. We assume responsibility for our relationships and therefore we control the destiny of each one.

Once we have clarity on what we want for ourselves, we can relate to others in a unique, stable, harmonious and magnificent way. But everything depends on our inner reality, which consists of our emotions, desires and thoughts. Because thoughts are creative, they create everything around us, especially those things that they focus on and comprehend. Sometimes it happens consciously, but in most cases, it is an unconscious process. If we want to change our world and our relationships, we must simply begin by changing our thoughts.

THE INNER MIRROR

In order to properly carry out this visualization exercise, find a quiet spot, relax your body and quiet your thoughts. Imagine a large white screen with a giant mirror in your mind. In that mirror, reflect the image of your significant other or the person for whom you feel an attraction. Once you can clearly see this picture, project onto the image everything that you love about that other person, and everything that causes conflicts for you in the relationship.

When you see something in your partner's behavior that has upset you, stop for a moment to think about what exactly has upset you. Once your ideas are clear, explain them to your partner, as though the mirror were a scene from real life. Once you've clearly identified that annoying defect or behavior in your partner, you'll realize that it is also a defect or behavioral pattern that you reject in yourself.

The more you practice this exercise the more you will realize that love is just like this mirror. The universe that we create around ourselves depends upon the way we see things. And this is without a doubt the result of our vision of love.

The most important thing to consider before entering into any relationship is your first love: the love that you feel for yourself.

Liberating Ourselves from False Mirrors and Relationships

This next exercise helps us to understand how we cling to the images that others have of us, and how important it is to love ourselves unconditionally. This visualization will connect you with the false image that you have of yourself, and will lead you to appreciate yourself more.

Visualize a great gallery filled with corridors. Walk until you come to a room in which the walls are totally covered by mirrors of different sizes and shapes. Take your time observing how you feel. Stop in front of the mirror that you most identify with. Note which one you choose, because every aspect of yourself that you discover while you're being reflected in your inner mirror is part of you. These may be familiar to you, or they may not be; for example, you may observe that the person in the mirror is passive, emotionless and very still, yet you consider yourself active and emotionally open to your partner. It's possible that you don't accept these hidden aspects of your personality as a true part of yourself. It is possible, then, that you may be bothered by these qualities in others, or that you attract people into your life that seem like they don't offer enough. It's important for you to relate to these inner parts of your-self, understand them and try to identify what they need. Create an inner dialogue that will allow you to know these aspects more fully, until you no longer find yourself rejecting these characteristics in yourself. If you can accept every aspect of your inner self, your rela-tionship with your partner will be more harmonious.

Focus your attention on the living brilliance of your eyes, and notice how beautiful they are. Realize that they are the reflection of your soul, always radiating inside you. Feel how your soul needs to love you. As you vibrate with that love and splendor, you will real-ize how important you are to yourself—so much so that you may no longer need approval or validation from others.

When we feel affection, respect and conscious acceptance of our-selves, this will be reflected in our bodies and we will transmit this loving energy to the world around us. Learning to think positively about yourself is directly connected to knowing yourself, identifying your qualities and flaws, and accepting yourself so that you can pos-itively transform your life.

People who love themselves are genuinely ready to begin a rela-tionship. They manage their emotions and inner issues intelligently. For example, they

- Maintain a calm attitude in the face of stimuli.
- Lean on their partners and allow the other to rely on them, without creating dependence.
- Are dedicated to growing.
- Commit to what they say and do.
- Handle breakups and separations with maturity.
- Control their language.
- Learn to read subliminal messages from people that they want to influence on an emotional level.
- Discuss their feelings in the relationship without fear of losing their partner.
- Evaluate the emotions they provoke in others.

- Know the difference between what they feel and what their mind is seeking.
- Know their true feelings and can distinguish them from other people's expectations.
- Fall in love with someone who will reciprocate.
- Perform sex in a natural and loving manner.
- Attract people with similar aspirations, with the likelihood of having the fewest conflicts.
- Are capable of listening to criticism without taking it personally, because negative messages have little power over them.

These elements keep us centered, allowing us to observe and react to the changes that take place around us without becoming negatively affected by them.

Once we understand the law of attraction as a magnetized mirror that attracts all that we think and are, we must also learn to love ourselves and to understand that relationships are made up of stages, mannerisms, contracts and power exchanges. When these aspects are known and respected, the relationship produces maximum enjoyment and satisfaction, generating absolute happiness.

There are as many forms of love as there are relationships. Every human being is capable of loving dozens of people, each in a different way, and every one of those relationships may correctly be described by the word *love*. This book examines relationship models and their characteristics, and how to optimize our own relationships after saying "I love you."

CHAPTER 2

I Love You and
I'm Falling Deeper in Love

Love is an unexplored mystery: new, undiscovered and foreign; we never know where it comes from and what remote refuge it escapes to when it departs.

Romance and Falling in Love

Regardless of our age or emotional situation, falling in love is one of the great miraculous possibilities that life offers us. It is a complex process, one that is much easier to feel than to describe. There are all kinds of theories on the subject. One defines falling in love as an altered state of consciousness in which our attitudes and emotions are out of control, magically driving us to experience significant changes in our perception of things.

Scientists who study the dynamics of the brain are intrigued by the changes produced on a cerebral level when a person falls in love. They have discovered that when a person feels the ecstasy of being attracted to another, the brain produces elevated quantities of endorphins—substances produced by specialized neurons located in the central region of the brain known as the hypothalamus. These endorphins carry out a series of connections between neurons that affect our emotions, memory and learning, dreaming and waking states, as well as hunger.

As the endorphins increase, a person may experience loss of appetite, see things through "rose-colored glasses" and feel as though he or she is floating in a state of extreme happiness and euphoria.

But why do we fall in love with one specific person and not with another? What is so special about that one person that makes our hypothalamus secrete such substances?

A great number of theories attempt to answer these questions. Some maintain that we have imprinted in our unconscious the image of our progenitors, and we seek those who resemble them. This applies in particular to the ancestor of the opposite sex, because that ideal of man or woman is the one we grew up with.

Many of us fall in love with someone who possesses some personality trait that we ourselves yearn to have. Sometimes this trait is attractive to us at the beginning of the relationship, but later on we may actually reject it. When we are young, we often fall for people with whom we identify in some way, because that feels safer.

Emotions Produced at the Beginning of a Romantic Relationship

When we begin a relationship with someone and fall in love, we're in an emotional state of joy and happiness. When people are in love, it affects their body language, the way they look at and listen to their partner and the way they smile at them. It's as though they have a special light shining in their eyes.

Falling in love produces pleasure. All of our senses become more receptive: we are suddenly capable of detecting subtle changes in tone of voice, gaze and gesture. We allow ourselves to fully experience our emotions, and our entire organism is revitalized by it. It also increases our self-esteem. We feel more confident and more important; we feel loved. Even those aspects of ourselves that we don't like become less important. It is as though magic had occurred: the mirror in which we see ourselves reflected every day to find our defects and flaws has now become a source of praise in which everything is beautiful and perfect.

Falling in love is not something we do voluntarily. It cannot be created or be made to disappear. It either exists or it doesn't.

Don't Be Afraid to Love

When you set out to embrace the concept of loving with freedom, you've broken through the inner barrier of fear. You will feel your emotions freely, and you will suddenly understand others more.

Angel is a clear example of somebody who fears initiating a relationship and losing one's freedom. This fear is very common because many people feel that entering a relationship requires losing one's individuality. Angel admits:

I was afraid and now I realize it was love. I confessed to my friend on the faculty via email that I was in love with her:

"I want to stay beside you and give you everything you need to be happy. That way I will be happy as well. . . . Through the freedom that only love can give you, the freedom to choose whom to love. . . . I want to perceive that aroma of freedom that I can breathe only when you are beside me, because what I am breathing and what is sustaining me is love. Now you have the freedom to choose whether that love that is on this side of the mirror, on this side of the window, on this side of the world, is inside of you as well. I will be waiting for you,

Your Angel

I cite this example because it's so beautiful: Angel understood the need for true love and his partner accepted the challenge.

A romantic relationship is perfect when it is understood from the beginning that every day is a choice, a discovery, a new sensation. When a relationship starts out as a sincere and careful awakening to what we are, to what we desire, to our own history and our own projects, this is the perfect place in which to know what roles we are able to play in relating to others and to know within what limits and according to what set of principles we are able to enact them.

Anxiety and Falling in Love

Although the case I just mentioned involves a couple that enjoyed an emotional, physical and spiritual attraction, not all people seek a partner purely out of love. Some people seek a partner just to cover their own shortcomings or because they don't want to be alone. This can lead to frustration, confusion and unrequited love.

When people enter into a relationship, negative feelings can arise. These inner manifestations are uncontrollable unless we become conscious of them. Typically, a problem within a relationship is not caused because the partners are wrong for each other; the conflict actually resides inside each individual.

The trouble with human beings is that everybody thinks about changing humanity, while almost nobody thinks about changing themselves. Nonetheless, even those who already accept the fact that change begins at the personal level seek it outside of themselves.

Below are some of the most common feelings that people experience as a result of hiding their anxiety about intimacy or love. We all manifest this behavior, consciously or unconsciously, at some point or another in our lives, especially when entering a relationship. Let's look at how it's possible to modify this. Pay attention as you read and consider whether any of these impulses apply to you.

The Drive for Perfection and Virtue: These people get lost in obsessive perfectionism, in details. All of their thoughts are self-critical.

All of their attention is focused primarily on what doesn't agree with their idea of virtue and perfection, so that they can criticize it and correct it.

The person's thought base is: "We have to fix this, it's not working, it's not perfect, it's wrong."

This type of individual feels that his or her life is lacking in something, and often feels out of control. The important thing here is to learn how to relax and live in the present. Try not to project your personal frustrations onto your partner.

The Desire to Be Loved: All of us carry the basic desire for love, but when this impulse is driven by fear of losing one's partner, it becomes an obsession. The fear leads to emotional manipulation and compulsive generosity. It is often experienced by people who love too much and control everything their partner does. They are attuned to people who love easily, offering satisfaction in order to feel indispensable and superior to others.

The thought base: "They have to love me, I give them everything."

For the person suffering from this compulsive desire, it is best to find a solution by improving his or her own self-esteem outside the relationship. The best thing to do is to concentrate on yourself; pursue your own hobbies and interests and focus on improving your own life.

The Need for Security: Everyone feels a basic need to feel secure in relationships, but when security becomes the main focus of an individual's attention, the relationship will become a dull routine and the trust between the partners may deteriorate. People who put all their energy into security feel the need to adhere very strictly to a framework of belief systems, institutions and schedules. They focus their attention on discovering potential attacks or signs of impending catastrophes, in order to be prepared. They desire to be protected against the world. For this reason, their behavior is often combative, defiant, but they don't want to abandon their security, as that is their most complex issue to resolve. Most wars are rooted in this impulse. Thousands of daily conflicts between couples are fixed or blocked by this drive, the search for security, the need to defend oneself from instability. Many unhappy married couples will stay together for years because of it, bringing only misfortune upon themselves.

The thought base: "What I possess gives me security and I am safe, and I must defend it at all costs."

Romance and love cannot endure when based in these types of negative desires, just as the body cannot be healthy with a nutritional base filled with toxins. The only way to break the cycle is to know our own desires and to know that the mind traps us in its many labyrinths.

What Do We Do If Love Really Does Show Up?

We spend a large portion of our lives searching for and waiting to be found by that "someone special." So, what happens when that person finally shows up?

In the case of thirty-year-old Sammy, love just showed up and surprised her. She had a very special friend from childhood whom she had always seen as the perfect mate, but never dared to expose her feelings. Yet one special day, he confessed his love:

That sentence was unforgettable. Aside from making me get a lump in my throat, it gave me hope . . . So I'm confused. When he told me "I love you," I felt such pressure in my chest, a huge smile on my face and my eyes all glassy from holding back tears of joy . . . After that, it was very touching—my face was like that of a teenager in love and I'd get embarrassed. I don't think of myself as the typical woman in love.

Over time, every time he'd say, "I love you," which used to excite every fiber of my being, began turning into an everyday thing.

"I love you." Obviously this phrase must be preceded by several

expressions of commitment that will vary in their intensity as the level of enjoyment and the need increases. But the most significant expression that we can hope for—verbally speaking, of course—is to find ourselves hearing those three tiny little words.

For Sammy, falling in love helped her overcome her confusion and fear.

Falling in love requires us to conquer the habit of having our world centered entirely around ourselves, and this always causes a certain amount of pain. That's why everybody complains about love but still longs for it.

Experiencing love means risking your ego, and that can lead to hurt. Now the ego has to share things, feelings, ideas, opinions, spaces, money and time. The ego is like a small child who doesn't want to share toys with his siblings, friends or companions; he wants everything for himself.

Here are some suggestions to help you be more alert to your blocks against going on with a relationship, and maintaining the initial spark of love:

- View the relationship as though you are both moving to a new territory and must also learn a new language. In this case, both should move into the other's territory, and not expect only one partner to adapt.
- Accept the differences between partners and respect them; don't try to unify yourselves into one being with only one mind and heart.
- Differences between lovers can become a source of mutual knowledge and growth.
- Use the relationship and all the newness that it offers as a means to nourish yourselves as individuals.
- There will always be parts of one another's personalities that each considers essential and this will allow the pair to live in harmony as equals.

- Don't try to hide the parts that you most dislike about yourself, because in the end this will only cause your partner to end up disliking those aspects of you as well.
- We all have to express our needs. Don't wait for your partner to read your mind; say how you feel and ask for what you want.
- Don't try to change your partner to be more like you, as this will ultimately destroy the relationship; it's a waste of your energy to focus on your partner instead of trying to improve yourself. Be tolerant of the problems within the relationship, but do not tolerate things that make you feel untrue to your own principles.
- Believe in your partner; not doing so implies not believing in your own choice of a partner or in your feelings regarding yourself.
- Love is a process that takes time. Attraction and falling in love happen very spontaneously, but true love requires cultivation.
- When a couple falls in love, they will inevitably evolve and change. We cannot expect that the person we love will always be as he or she is right now.
- Accept the fact that after the very intense period of passion during the onset of your relationship, a period of less intensity may follow.
- The search for love leads nowhere. You cannot go out searching for love. Anyone who searches has to take responsibility for what he or she finds. What we cannot anticipate is who, when, how or at what price.
- When you're in a relationship, realize that you can give everything beautiful inside yourself and everything beautiful that you are, but you cannot take on the responsibility for your partner's happiness.
- Finding a partner is not the final destination in love's journey. It is only the beginning.
- When you don't see eye to eye, don't attempt to convince your partner of your point of view. You just think differently and you

have different objectives in mind. Respecting these differences is the foundation for mature communication.

- Every day ask yourself if you would still choose the same partner again. Ask yourself this question without fear, as it is a healthy question for both partners to explore. Boredom and dissatisfaction result when one is not able or willing to ask this question.
- Love is nourishment, a beautiful landscape; it is action and reception, a permanent cycle of planting and harvesting.

Entering into a relationship has a lot to do with our manner of sharing affection with others, which we have developed over time through different satisfying bonds of affection, particularly those experienced with our families. Every time we fall in love, the models and expectations that we drag around with us from our earliest experiences are all present. Relationships often fail because the partners unconsciously repeat failed models from earlier relationships, or familial ones, or because one expects the other to fill some sort of void left over from a previously unsatisfying emotional experience. How many times have we heard people say, "If I had known what I was getting into, I would never have gotten married"? But what is it that one should have known? To put it a bit bluntly: that your partner is not the Prince Charming or the perfect lover/mother that you imagined at the onset of love? There may be exceptions, to be sure, but hardly anybody totally fulfills the expectations that he or she first inspires in a partner during the early stages of falling in love.

During the romantic phase, we excuse everything because we're "living in a bubble." It's good to stand back and reflect a little here. Perhaps we could set up a trial living arrangement or committed relationship in which we could actually demonstrate what expectations we have for each other. We can make our decision afterward, always leaving the door open to changes and unforeseen circumstances, because feelings and love can't be planned. Sometimes surprises happen, and often these are great blessings that open our eyes to reality.

Before making a formal commitment, such as marriage, it's important to test the relationship in a way that will allow us to get to know our partner on a deeper level, understanding his or her way of thinking and behaving on a daily basis. This will also enable us to explore how we perceive other people, what is expected from him or her and what each of us must give in order to make the other happy and to consolidate the relationship.

CHAPTER 3

I Love You and I Want You to Feel Sure of My Love

I am inebriated by your eyes and want to sip on your kisses eternally. My soul experiences a sweet enchantment when I embrace you, like flying without wings, far beyond time and space. I travel to a place so unique and secure that my mind rests and retires there. In that zone, without limits, I feel the nearness of your skin, and my heart vibrates with a delightful melody that is neither from the heavens nor from the earth.

I am so in love with you that I have declared my love for you without words, in total silence.

How Do We Know When It's Love?

How many couples in the first romantic stages of the relationship make promises of love to one another? Little commitments are made from the bottom of one's heart, because in the moment, no one else exists but that other person. Some reflect intense desires filled with passion, while others are a bit more thought out. This can lead to one of these typical dialogues later on:

"Do you love me?" she asks.

"Yes," he answers.

"No, I mean, really?" she insists.

"Yes, darling, seriously."

"And how long will you go on loving me?"

"Forever."

"How do you know that you really love me?" she asks, feeling unsure of herself.

"That's not something you know, it's something you feel," he affirms confidently.

"And how do you know if what you're feeling is love?"

"First of all, I miss you when you're not around."

"You can miss your friends, your cat, your coworker, your dad," she replies.

"Yes, but I also think about you all day long. I imagine you by my side, in the future, in five years, ten years, maybe even fifty years down the road, growing old together and baby-sitting our grandchildren."

"Really?" she asks.

"Yes, it's really love. Don't question it."

"And is it still love when we argue?"

"We argue because we're human beings. We can't possibly agree on 100 percent of all things 100 percent of the time. Even when we argue, I still feel so many beautiful feelings toward you, although you really try my patience."

"Thanks."

"I love you. Don't worry, darling," he affirms. "I know that I love you because you give me everything that I ever dreamed of. Everything I've always been searching for: stability, peace, harmony. Life became more simple and clear when I met you," he concludes.

Love is so brilliant and simple that it expects us to believe that someone loves us, because, really, there's no concrete way to prove it.

Following this reflection on romance and true love, I ran into a good friend of mine, Daniel, who is forty-five years old. After going through several relationships, even marriage, he's still searching for love. He told me about how he felt about a beautiful woman whom he had met only a few weeks earlier:

I woke up the other night, and being so used to waking up alone, I found her in my bed instead. She looked so beautiful next to me with her eyes closed. I felt right then and there that I wanted to spend the remainder of my days, my entire life, with her. I woke her up with a kiss and caressed her entire body. I made love to her for an hour then said, "Marry me." Her reaction was a little frightened, almost trembling, and she answered, "You're a beautiful person but we should wait awhile, since we just met."

Women are more intelligent and sometimes much more realistic than men. I would surrender my whole life to her right now. Why wait?

I replied, "I agree that you should wait." We smiled and continued talking about love and people in love.

I think that emotions are beautiful, but the heart, in order to maintain its pure and joyful deliverance to another human being, needs to be like a child in the womb. It needs a period of time to mature, a period of time in which to be born and all the time in the world to live.

How Do You Declare Your Love?

This is one of the most exciting moments in your relationship, and one that provokes such anxiety that at any age, one feels the same set of fears, insecurities or romantic desire, butterflies in the stomach and one thousand sensations and thoughts all at once.

Women used to have to wait for the man to declare his love first. Nowadays, women have become more assertive. Nonetheless, many still wait instead of choosing to take the initiative. Are you one of these women? It's important to place yourself on the same level as men and learn to affirm your love. That is why in this section we refer to men and women in the same role.

There are many innovative and fun ways to declare your love, but you should prepare the right ambience for intimacy beforehand. Here are some suggestions for facilitating a romantic encounter:

First, lead the conversation toward topics related to love and romance, for example:

- Start a conversation in which you point out all of the areas in which you are compatible. Emphasize the similarities and overlook the differences.
- You may begin with a story about some movie you saw that reminds you of your relationship. Tell him or her how you've always dreamed of a relationship such as the one you share, and describe some of the most important and special moments that you have experienced together, especially the day you met.
- If you're not shy, you might try saying, "I had an erotic dream," and you'll be on the right track.
- In order to establish light physical contact, observe the following details: maintain eye contact at all times as you prepare for the moment when you will say, "I love you." Hold his or her hand or gently caress his or her face.
- While expressing some affectionate gesture, say something flattering, for instance: "I love your eyes, the way you look at me, your skin, your voice . . ." Point out details that you are especially fond of.
- Another fun thing to do is to learn to say "I love you" in some foreign language and repeat it before kissing. This way, your partner can figure out the meaning.
- Another way of declaring your love is to give your beloved a book of poems. Before presenting the gift, take the time to

highlight all of the phrases or lines that you identify with. You can even decorate the pages with hearts or cute stickers. This act demonstrates tenderness, and nobody can resist such sweetness.

- Make up an intriguing anecdote. For instance, tell him or her that your first meeting felt like déjà vu. This always works. After you've been dating awhile, you can confess that it was merely a ploy to create a special moment between the two of you.

WHERE TO SAY "I LOVE YOU"

- Either of you can invite the other to dine at home. Decorate the bathroom mirror with either lipstick or shaving cream that spells out *I Love You*. This lovely detail can conquer any human being, including the toughest at heart.
- Invite the person to a beach or a lake, depending on the season, and surprise him or her by writing "I Love You" in the sand.
- Invite him or her to a wedding if you happen to have friends who are getting married during this period. It's an ideal and romantic moment to say "I love you."
- In the car: invite the person for a drive somewhere remote and tranquil. Play a recording of a song that has some romantic meaning for the two of you and say that it's a surprise you want him or her to hear.
- Create a romantic blog with your two names in it and send your beloved an e-mail to announce the surprise. Include pictures of the two of you. You can ask him or her for some pictures or shoot some during a special occasion.
- Cyberspace has bridged the gap between those who are shy and those who are less so. If you're into chatting online together, you can even declare your love in the chat room and send along an electronic kiss with a little icon that means "I love you."

The Language of Kisses

The moment you say "I love you," it is essential to seal and affirm your statement with the most direct form of communication: the kiss. What can be said about a kiss that millions of poets, artists and musicians have not already expressed? In actuality, kissing has its own language.

Kissing someone provokes a series of different reactions and allows us to express many emotions. With just a simple kiss, you may discover what your partner wants to communicate with you, turning that simple act into a means of fulfilling your partner's desires.

Kisses are subject to a wide variety of circumstances, but certain types of kisses imply different things:

Kiss on the cheek: transmits affection, support and complicity, regardless of physical attraction.

Kiss on the lips: implies passion, may mean "I love you" or "I want to date you." If it is carried out very quickly, just barely touching one another's lips, it may mean simply friendship. This is why the intensity of the kiss is an important factor in interpreting its intention.

Kiss on the collarbone: implies intimacy and manifests a certain degree of erotic intention in the giver. It is a very effective seductive gesture.

Kiss on the ears: this gesture is charged with passionate sexual intention and power. It may be taken not too seriously, depending on the intensity with which the kiss is given. This kiss is imbued with the energy of play and mischief.

Kiss on the hands: either in women or men implies admiration, tenderness, or desire for love. Additionally, it expresses trust on the part of the giver.

Kiss accompanied by an embrace: when both bodies are in close contact, this is an expression of strong affection and surrender. Both are willing to give in to one another on both a sensual and a sexual level.

Kiss accompanied by an intense look of endearment: the person receiving the kiss feels tenderly loved, whether the kiss is on the face or the lips.

The Fire of Touch

Caresses are also important in seduction and are most effective when used just like kisses. By placing your hands all over your lover's body, you may awaken and direct passion with all of the intensity that you dare to express. When the caress is used consciously, in all its variations, you may easily perceive the other's energy, emotion and capacity for love. A caress does not end at the fingertips and its influence does not end at the surface of the skin. Using the language of touch, we are able to channel our vital and sexual force. People in Eastern cultures teach that there are four areas of the hand through which to transmit the fire of love, each with distinctive qualities of energy and physical sensations for the receptive partner.

• The fingertips
• The base of the fingers
• The palm of the hand
• The heel of the hand

Followers of Tantra affirm that they can feel the heat of the body as a vital fire that burns as we caress our partner. They also advise imagining, feeling or visualizing the energetic glow that emanates from our hands and fingers while we caress our partner or receive our partner's caresses. We can actually feel the two fires fusing together as the two bodies are joined. Once you freely practice the art of caressing your partner, you will discover your partner's desires and preferences and what areas of the body yield the greatest pleasure for him or her.

Twenty Quotations for Lovers

Romance is, without a doubt, the most reliable manner we have of connecting to our partner's body and feelings. In this way, we can demonstrate decisively our desire to surrender to our beloved. As a result we stimulate the creativity and passion that every relationship needs to keep the flame burning. It is an act of generosity to set aside time for romance, as this affirms the importance of the relationship and our partner to our lives. Romance is the healer of tensions between couples because it keeps alive the passion, emotion and energy of love inside of us.

Often on the first date we might have no idea what to say, and we fear that we'll sound tacky or too romantic. Later on, we may need some ideas for things to write in a love letter, inspiration for an anniversary card or a Valentine's Day e-mail, or perhaps a phrase that will break the ice or help us get back together after a quarrel. Below is a list of quotations that may help:

1. *Love is a flower / You got to let it grow.*—John Lennon
2. *Some people never say "I love you," yet they deeply desire to hear it.*—Paul Simon (paraphrased)
3. *A kiss is a lovely trick designed by nature to stop speech when words become superfluous.*—Ingrid Bergman
4. *A coward is incapable of exhibiting love; it is the prerogative of the brave.*—Mahatma Gandhi
5. *Love has nothing to do with what you are expecting to get—only what you are expecting to give—which is everything.*—Katharine Hepburn
6. *You can seduce a man without taking anything off, without even touching him.*—Rae Dawn Chong

7. *Your words are my food, your breath my wine. You are everything to me.*—Sarah Bernhardt

8. *I've been taught ever since I was a kid that sex is filthy and forbidden, and that's the way I think it should be. The filthier and more forbidden it is, the more exciting it is.*—Mel Brooks

9. *I have to be physically attracted to someone. But I can't just be with someone just because it's great sex. Because orgasms don't last long enough.*—Courteney Cox Arquette

10. *I love you, not only for what you are, but for what I am when I am with you.*—Roy Croft

11. *Caresses, expressions of one sort or another, are necessary to the life of the affections as leaves are to the life of a tree. If they are wholly restrained, love will die at the roots.*—Nathaniel Hawthorne

12. *To love is to receive a glimpse of heaven.*—Karen Sunde

13. *Sex pleasure in woman is a kind of magic spell; it demands complete abandon; if words or movement oppose the magic of caresses, the spell is broken.*—Simone de Beauvoir

14. *Keep your love of nature, for that is the true way to understand art more and more.*—Vincent van Gogh

15. *I believe that imagination is stronger than knowledge, that myth is more potent than history, and dreams are more powerful than facts, that hope always triumphs over experience, that laughter is the only cure for grief, and that love is stronger than death.*—Robert Fulghum

16. *Love is a game that two can play and both win.*—Eva Gabor

17. *Whoever you are, now I place my hand upon you, that you be my poem; I whisper with my lips close to your ear, I have loved many women and men, but I love none better than you.*—Walt Whitman

18. *Falling in love is not at all the most stupid thing that people do—but gravitation cannot be held responsible for people falling in love.*—Albert Einstein

19. *We come to love not by finding a perfect person, but by learning to love an imperfect person perfectly.*—Sam Keen

20. *After all these years, I see that I was mistaken about Eve in the beginning; it is better to live outside the Garden with her than inside it without her.*—Mark Twain

This chapter discussed the romantic stage of a relationship and, ideally, this stage should last for the whole relationship. You will find a lot of advice in the remainder of this book on how to keep romance alive forever.

CHAPTER 4

I Love You a Thousand Ways

Every couple must experience the relationship as a journey whose destiny is to fulfill a true and committed love. The seasons are the stages within the relationship, but they also create the path, and every moment within the relationship is a season to be enjoyed.

Relationship Models and Testimonials

Courtship is one of the most beautiful stages of a relationship, as it encourages love, happiness and stability. The ideal during this stage is to find respect, reciprocity, knowledge of one another, acceptance, and detachment from the self. Courtship is the training ground for love. This is the perfect time for establishing your desires before entering a more stable or committed relationship. Communicate your concerns and explore your capacity for solving problems together and negotiating agreements. This is also the time to let go of one's idealized notions about the relationship, to look at one another's flaws and virtues, and to see one another as real people and not as fairy-tale characters.

The three factors that contribute to the ultimate success of a relationship are intimacy, passion and commitment. The absence of any one of these factors is at the root of many failed relationships, because the success of a couple requires an equilateral triangle combining the three: intimacy, passion and commitment. Intimacy allows the relationship to last. It includes communication, surrender, respect, emo-

30

tional support and the desire to promote the well-being of the other. During intimacy we learn who we are; here we reflect on and determine strategies dictating our behavior in relation to our partner, as well as our parents, children, coworkers and others that we interact with. An intimate space is also where we share the circumstances and beliefs that order our lives. If we don't set aside time for being alone with our mate, we stand to lose the intimacy that is so crucial to our relationship. The trick is to find a perfect balance between intimacy and autonomy.

Passion is basically the intense desire to unite with a partner: a sense of belonging, an expression of desire and need, and sexual satisfaction.

Commitment is the decision to love someone and maintain that love. It is the conviction that the success of the relationship is a lifelong project worthy of striving for, a promise to weather the crises and external circumstances working against love.

Listed below are seven points that reflect upon a healthy relationship and synthesize the three essential factors.

1. Each member of the couple must maintain a constant intention to fulfill the other's needs.
2. Each partner must learn to determine when to give in to the other's desires.
3. Love your partner as he or she truly is and not as your idealized version of him or her.
4. Learn how to tolerate anything that cannot be changed.
5. Be sincere with one another.
6. Enjoy good times and grow together in the face of difficulties.
7. Treat your partner the way you would like to be treated.

There are different types of committed relationship models that are important to become aware of in order to become more familiar with your own. Romantic relationships touch our soul deeply, even though many times they do not end up lasting. Even if we may not realize it until the relationship ends, relationships are genuine love stories.

The Romantic Relationship

This relationship model occurs when the emotional and physical attraction is complete and the two partners reach a level of harmony. Often, however, things do not deepen beyond this point and the couple decides to break up before making a commitment. The relationship remains frozen in time and often becomes idealized, leaving one or both partners disappointed and affecting their ability to move forward with their lives.

A relationship can move past the initial stage only if we overcome certain blocks in ourselves that we had never dealt with before. After the period of idyllic bliss, a couple can actually develop a real relationship, as in the case of Juan, age 27:

I never imagined that I was such a romantic. In fact, I was one of those guys who didn't even believe in love. Then one night I met her in a bar. I asked for her e-mail address so as not to seem too forward. I sent her a bunch of sweet messages and we carried on for a month like that. During that time I felt something special for her; she had become very important to me. Since we didn't know each other very well yet, I could tell her my entire life story without fear, and she could tell me hers. One day I decided to give her my phone number and asked her for hers. Her answer was very direct: she would give it to me "at the right time."

One evening, to my great surprise, I answered the phone and there she was. She had a beautiful voice and was just as sweet by phone as she had been by e-mail. I had no idea what to say, as everything seemed so strange and was happening so quickly. When I checked my e-mail, I found a message from her. In it, she gave me her phone number. I didn't waste any time and called her right away. Two months passed between the first time we wrote to one another and today. What I felt for her had gone from simple affection to something much stronger, almost indescribable. When we saw each other, it was magical. I had butterflies in my stomach and my heart was pounding in my chest. At first, we simply said hello and gave each other a little peck on the cheek and a small hug. From that point on, everything was marvelous. She's the love of my life and I fell completely in love. She's everything to me. This is the most important thing that has happened in my life and I can honestly say that I really am in love, without a doubt.

Juan's case is a fine example of how love can transform us into more loving and angelic beings than we ever imagined ourselves to be.

The Conflictive Relationship

People sometimes come together when they feel some affinity regarding problems. Moving in together can also provide an escape from economic or personal conflicts with one's primary family. Many relationships are also formed by people who are both lonely. Yet in these cases neither person is taking into account what the other person is really like. This type of relationship is very common, but most couples are unaware of it.

Staying in love requires a commitment to learning one another's idiosyncrasies and learning to communicate and resolve conflicts. It's about helping one another mutually and sharing, without fear of losing love. Naturally, it is very difficult for any relationship that grows out of conflict to end up being positive.

Heather, age twenty-eight, is aware that she sought a relationship to escape her own conflicts:

We were a bit young when we got married. We had a conflictive relationship. We both needed to escape from our families, or at least that was the subject we talked about most often. We felt bonded by our shared problems somehow—that was our point of connection—and both of us felt it intuitively.

I still have a lot of unresolved feelings. I don't understand his lack of understanding. In spite of everything that happened to us, I feel hurt. He never knew how to really listen to me. Actually, both of us are hurt.

We were selfish with one another. The pain in my soul has healed, but I still have to deal with the wounds in my heart—the ones produced by his words and mine. I don't want to blame him for everything. When we were married, somehow I was always confused by his mood swings. He wasn't like that when we were dating. He changed later on, and became more aggressive while I got very defensive. I think that deep down inside, we are such similar people. I feel like I'm dying. I am so afraid of being without him.

These are, among other things, some of the thoughts that still linger in my head. I couldn't say them to him because of the hatred, the rage and the love that was generated during a difficult moment. Anyway, I pray to God that he'll lead him down the right path in life. Let him decide what will become of him. I'm grateful for both the good and bad things that we went through, though.

One additional comment: I learned something even from our worst times together. To me, this means that our journey together in life was always positive. It is absolutely impossible for love to cause suffering. You suffer over things you lack and emotional traumas from your childhood. Many believe that they're experiencing the love of their lives because they're sacrificing themselves and abandoning their own lives. To say love causes suffering is entirely contradictory; happiness does not cause suffering.

Generally, in this type of relationship, one can see a game of mirrors happening: two people reflecting one another's conflicts. If you are in a relationship and you are not receiving the love that you desire, you should start to look for a solution, but not in your partner; look inside yourself.

Each partner in the couple reflects the other's internal states. It is often easier to blame the other person and want him or her to change than it is to change ourselves. We're consoled by thinking that they've got more flaws than we do and we cover up the real problem: a low level of self-esteem, not opening oneself to the love that one desires.

The couple's functionality depends upon the self-esteem of its members. If your thoughts are negative, you can expect to attract someone with the same problems. The work I describe in this book in the section on the inner mirror (pp. 6–7) is very useful for resolving conflicts and strengthening the positive aspects of each partner's personality.

LOW SELF-ESTEEM COUPLE

When one partner in a couple is suffering from low self-esteem, the other one will also suffer, because everything in a relationship is a reflection. In this case, the consciousness of the couple as well as the possibility for growth is limited.

Here is how to recognize if one of the partners is suffering from low self-esteem:

- The person tends to avoid problems in the relationship or his personal life, and one partner is unaware of what the other desires or needs.
- One partner is constantly comparing himself to the other, and this leads to feelings of unrest.
- This partner mistrusts the other and creates childish games in the relationship, from scenes of unreasonable jealousy to senseless conflicts.
- The person relates to his partner without a genuine, honest commitment, or directly seeks outside casual relationships. The natural expression of feelings is blocked; the person may be ignoring his feelings, avoiding them or feeling ashamed of them.
- The person lacks clear and defined values and agreements; there is constant confusion in his judgments regarding the relationship as well as toward himself.
- The person cannot accept personality differences and compulsively wants to mold his partner into his own image and likeness.
- The person avoids communication and withdraws during a conflict. He neither wants nor is able to communicate what is hap-

pening to him because he doesn't know what he wants. He encourages emotional, financial or sexual dependence from his partner or becomes dependent himself.
• One partner consistently disrespects or invades the other's personal space.

Below are fifteen rules for anyone who wishes to rise above these patterns and seek a positive relationship with oneself and with others:

1. Establish the rules regarding what you need before committing to a relationship.
2. Don't get into relationships with the intention of changing the person later on.
3. If what you are looking for is a commitment, don't set yourself up for failure in relationships that offer only casual sex.
4. If the person truly interests you, don't hold back from clearly expressing your expectations.
5. When you find the person you've been searching for, allow yourselves to be vulnerable with each other.
6. Find a partner whom you can trust and who will support and accept you.
7. Don't waste too much time worrying about what may have happened in the past, nor about what might happen in the future. Concentrate on the present.
8. Consider yourself equal to any other person, even if you recognize differences in specific talents, prestige, profession or economic standing.
9. Accept the fact that you are interesting and valuable to others, at least to those with whom you want to associate.
10. Recognize your negative personality traits and don't be ashamed of them. Try to transform them without repressing them.

11. Enjoy different types of activities with each other, such as relating amorously without conflicts, working, resting, walking, spending time with friends and so forth. Real intimacy is satisfying and exciting.
12. Don't seek out relationships for the purpose of escaping your inner conflicts.
13. Respect the feelings and lifestyles of others.
14. Accept compliments and attention from others. Don't ignore them. Do not behave with indifference toward others.
15. Take a few classes or workshops and read books on improving self-esteem and maintaining a positive attitude.

How to End Conflictive Relationships

Many people are incapable of expressing what has made them fall in love and choose a particular person. They simply feel a special attraction toward them. But it is even more difficult to explain the fact that a person can fall in love with someone whom he or she later ends up describing as "the wrong one." Nevertheless, many people end up falling for someone very similar to their ex-partner and having the same set of conflicts and problems. What causes this?

People tend to relate to their significant other as adults in ways that are similar to the ways in which they related to their parents as children. If their relationship with their parents was healthy, balanced and satisfying, they'll tend to look for partners that create similarly satisfying relationships.

On the other hand, when their relationship with their parents was unsatisfying and conflictive, they'll re-create this relationship model. It's as though this person were looking for a second chance to finally make things turn out another way. Thus, they choose partners in life with whom they may play out situations similar to the ones they experienced as children.

Once they reach this point of conflict, both members of the couple feel disillusioned with the other person. Each feels that the person has fooled him, that she is different from the way she seemed initially. In reality, they're not so different at all, but probably at the beginning, they were relating to one another in healthier ways. Once their fear was activated, they began to relate to one another through fear, following the inadequate patterns that they learned as children. In order to avoid and end this vicious cycle, both partners need to overcome their fears. The best way to do so is within the relationship, where it is easier for each to learn what he or she needs to change.

Naturally, to achieve this, it's necessary to get to know oneself as well as the other person, and to know the specific fears that each one has and the patterns of behavior associated with those fears that developed during childhood. This way, they can realize what they're doing when repeating some past pattern. Partners can then negotiate better behavior for dealing with those difficult moments to break the cycle of repetition by overcoming their deeply rooted childhood issues.

So, you've tried everything to improve the relationship but the problems just continue. You are totally convinced that your relationship is negative. The solution is: if you cannot modify the relationship, it is possible that you are the one who must change.

The following questions will help you analyze your behavioral patterns when relating to others and help you to decide whether they should be different.

- How was your relationship with your mother during your childhood?
- How was your relationship with your father during your childhood?
- How have your other romantic relationships been, and how have they been similar to the ones you had with your parents?
- What conflicts and problems do you tend to relive with your partner? What fears do you have that may be contributing to the emergence of these conflicts?

- Is there some conflict or pattern that has repeated itself several times or in all of your romantic relationships?
- What is the similarity between this conflict and the ones you experienced with your parents?

Based on your responses, what do you need to learn and do to overcome your fears and change the way you relate to others?

Evaluate Your Relationship

If you've answered all of these questions and are still not clear about whether your relationship is toxic and whether you should break it off, it is important that you do this evaluation.

- Do you feel that your relationship is not changing in spite of all your efforts?
- When your partner is feeling depressed or sick and you offer help, are you blocked from actually being able to do anything?
- Do you feel that everything that goes wrong in your relationship is your fault?
- Are there any subjects that you cannot bring up with your partner and that you have to keep hidden?
- Do you criticize or feel criticized often in the relationship?
- Do your conflicts with your partner always end up the same way? Because:
  1. Dialogue is not possible.
  2. Each partner does what he or she feels like doing, without taking into consideration the other's feelings.
  3. You cannot reach an agreement and end up yelling to the point of exhaustion.
  4. During arguments, one of the partners assumes the role of victim.
  5. You give in to your partner's wishes just to avoid further conflict.

6. You frequently remember doing things you wish you hadn't done and become infuriated with yourself.

If after reviewing these questions, you realize that you face these situations regularly, then it is possible that your relationship is toxic.

How do you identify a toxic relationship? In the same way that the body is affected by toxins, or poisons, that deteriorate its physical condition, relationships may also contain emotional toxins that affect it in a negative way. These may be deeply rooted defense mechanisms. The mind, while guarding against the natural process of falling in love, may generate toxic energy as a mechanism of resistance. The cause of these toxic emotions is the repression or denial of natural emotions. They are then projected onto our relationships in ways that generate conflict. And the vicious emotional cycle continues, with conflict generating more toxic emotions.

Relationships may start out in a natural way, as friendships, romances or crushes. As we begin to feel more intimately involved with the other person, new feelings crop up. This process is totally natural, but if these emotions start creating conflict or anxiety and we're not clear on what is happening to us, we may project those inner conflicts onto the relationship.

The relationship then enters a period of deterioration that is manifested in different ways: misunderstandings, abandonment, fear of commitment and deceit. While all humans have individual characteristics, as do all relationships, some common trends occur at this point.

- Immature or childish reactions
- Not having a clear awareness of our needs, individuality or identity
- The inability to communicate or understand the other person
- Fear, anxiety, jealousy, envy or insecurity
- Resentments that are not being addressed
- The desire to control or influence others

This list includes the most common toxic emotions. There are certainly others, as different as people and their varied relationships.

Although love is the best-known defense against any ailment, be it physical or psychological, toxic emotions are even more harmful and dangerous than physical toxins. They can break down the metabolism of any relationship, no matter how great its potential may be.

When a relationship lacks openness, frankness, respect or equality in the right to think and act independently, when there is no individual freedom, no affection, desire, tenderness or consideration on the part of one toward the other, the relationship does not promise a very positive outcome.

Toxic relationships keep partners that attached to a partnership that no longer works.

Love is a very powerful force and if we don't know how to channel it, we can easily fall into bitter disagreements. The first thing one must realize is that the self-esteem of both partners is far too low in this type of relationship. The most dramatic factor is that this relationship model is extremely difficult to change.

In order to modify it, we must work internally and use affirmations to elevate our level of self-esteem. The negative situation can only be changed if one of the partners changes, triggering the other partner to follow suit. Otherwise, the relationship is doomed to be crushed by its own weight.

Personal and Intimate Inventory

The purpose of this exercise is to make a daily list of all the situations that cause us pain. Then make another list with the possible reason for these situations. Additionally, you should record under what circumstances the same or a similar situation happened in your past.

Once you've worked on this inventory for a week, you can get a much clearer idea of your negative programming. In order to counter all those negative ideas, you must heal them by making a list of positive affirmations. Affirmations are among the most powerful tools of the human mind.

Below are a few suggestions. I recommend that you make a copy of this page. It's important to focus on the affirmation and visualize it clearly.

I, (your name), hereby affirm that . . .

- I love myself, no matter what happens.
- I deserve to have loving relationships.
- I forgive myself and others.
- I feel secure in sharing my emotions.
- I allow myself to think freely.
- I liberate myself from my past emotional conditioning.
- I am capable of asking for what I want and need in love.
- I have a right to have my desires fulfilled.
- I open my heart and accept others as they are.
- I am learning to listen to and trust my inner voice.

You can use this list or add your own phrases to it, according to your feelings and your situation. These affirmations will serve as a vote of confidence that you offer to yourself every day. Expect the blessings and satisfaction that your own spirit is ready and willing to offer you.

The ties that bind you are internal belief systems, regarding yourself and the world around you, but you can be liberated, because you already possess the key that opens the door to your happiness.

The Illusionary Relationship

This is one of the most frustrating types of relationships because people rush into marriage or commitment without going through the necessary process of getting to know one another and establishing intimacy. This is a relationship led by blind love in which each partner reflects their own desires, needs and expectations onto the other.

Amelia, age 25, shared with me her experience in an illusionary relationship. She projected all of her own fantasies, desires and needs onto her partner without taking the time to really get to know him. The expectation that someone will complete our lives, or that being in a couple will solve all of our problems, is a common misconception in this type of relationship. Learn to distinguish what you want to receive in a relationship from what the other person is actually prepared to offer.

Amelia confessed to me that she met her husband, thought she was in love and married him. She and her husband have since been separated for ten months:

After this experience with my husband I arrived at some conclusions—because I learned a lot and I plan to put these things into practice in my next relationship. I learned that love is that which I know, believe and want, but I also learned what I don't want. I don't believe in finding someone to fill our lives; I believe we need to be whole within ourselves in order for someone who is healthy and self-fulfilled to share his happiness with me.

I believe that love lives inside of us—nobody generates it. We have to have enough courage to develop and maintain it so that this can later manifest into two people who share thoughts and feelings. I don't believe in love at first sight or in believing in someone without having known him for a long time. Everything takes time. Even the rivers that converge on their way to the ocean, it's all a process of fluid connection. Now I think about respect and sincerity. I believe in a mature love that grants each of us the space in which to grow together. Nobody belongs exclusively to anyone else. The two people choose each other freely. It's important to have love that is shared without pressure, without demands, without coercing anyone, as opposed to relationships that hold us back. I desire a relationship between two people who support each other mutually during hard times, who know how to read one another's feelings, who carry a smile in their hearts and who can rely on each other even without saying anything. I believe that love is the result of different worlds that share a single function within one shared vibration of mind, spirit, heart and emotions.

Amelia's experience is interesting because it's about reflecting, learning and not letting the experience of divorce or separation become a trauma or frustration but rather a life lesson. Amelia learned, through her unfortunate experience, what she wants and doesn't want in a future relationship.

The Total Relationship

This type of relationship is the ideal. In this situation, the couple feels attracted physically, emotionally and spiritually, and this produces the need and desire for commitment as an established partnership. Intimacy is developed gradually as the relationship grows, and it can continue to grow forever, although this growth moves more slowly in the early stages.

Joel, age twenty-eight, told me his story regarding the stages of his relationship:

I never imagined that that night I was going to meet the person I had dreamed about all my life. One day, while out dancing with a friend, I decided to ask a girl to dance. She penetrated my heart directly from the moment I met her. It was impossible to avoid; she had the key to all my feelings. I had been looking for a girl who would be sweet, sensible, uncomplicated, intelligent and a dreamer; a girl I could totally be myself with, someone with whom I could discover and develop the best in each of us.

Our relationship went through several stages. We became very close friends; we exchanged hundreds of e-mail messages; we exchanged pictures and we talked on the phone. Her voice, her feelings, her ideas, her looks, her smile . . . I was feeling something that I had never imagined.

I told her I was falling in love with her, that I couldn't stop thinking about her. I wanted to be near her, to tell her that I loved her, to give her that kiss that I wanted so badly, that kiss that always died on my lips.

Then I heard her reply that she loved me too. For the first time in my life, I experienced love with the greatest intensity and felt loved in the same way back. We've spoken for hours since that day we met. We dated for several months and stayed together for two years. Then we decided to get married in order to continue sharing those special moments together. We've made a lot of plans. I want to marry her, I want her to achieve her goals in life and I want to be a part of her success and her entire life. In me, she'll have a great friend above all else: someone who will never leave her alone, someone who will give her all his understanding and support, and somebody who will love, respect and adore her above all things forever.

This compelling story illustrates the various hues of love.

The main thing to remember is what kind of relationship you are in from the beginning. Aim for a relationship of mutual learning and growth, in which the two of you can become better people than you already are.

CHAPTER 5

I Love You and
I Want to Live with You

If there is one thing that defines living together, it is the word sharing. Sharing only takes place when we fully and sincerely surrender something of ourselves, which paradoxically is not always something that can be divided in two.

The New Couple:
Living Together (A New Structure?)

Times have changed. The truth is that people are not as preoccupied with getting married as they once were. The fact that couples choose not to marry but to live together instead is creating a new structural model for relationships.

Many couples start out by spending a weekend together, and later, due to economic circumstances, especially in urban areas, they attempt to live together indefinitely. So essentially, whereas married couples of generations past were supported by the legality of the marriage contract and its binding commitments, many couples today cannot survive without maintaining a space for personal freedom, erotic compatibility and the mutual pleasure and satisfaction that two people who love each other are capable of bringing into one another's lives.

Today's couples know that they have at their disposal a multitude of alternatives to make their love lives more gratifying and lasting. They are also conscious of the fact that falling into a rut is their number-one enemy and that they cannot combat this in any other way than to explore new ways of experiencing erotic expression. Modern couples also expect friendship, trust, communication and freedom to express individual opinions within the relationship. By noting the trends in print and Internet articles, a profile for this modern couple emerges. Their average age is between twenty-five and thirty-eight. They tend to be professionals, independent, hedonistic, narcissistic and often have a high socioeconomic standing. They are avid consumers, lovers of new technology, travel and enjoy life's pleasures and who postpone having children to enjoy freedom, grow professionally and enjoy an eternal and blissful youth. This type of relationship is also common among people who had failed marriages early in life and, as a result, are afraid of committing to a new relationship.

In these relationships, as in all situations where a couple is living together over a period of time, certain conflicts arise that the couple must face, as easygoing as the relationship might be. In this type of relationship, couples often procrastinate when it comes to making important decisions. This may be related to their avoidance of other responsibilities such as marriage and having children. As Natalie, age twenty-six, explains:

Sometimes I don't know what to think. I started living with my boyfriend two years ago. I thought we were going to get married, so I moved into his apartment. The wedding is moving along slowly, but it's still on. I do love him, but lately things have been so difficult. Sometimes I have illusions and fantasies about my wedding, the party and the honeymoon, and even living together each day and starting a family. It feels like everything is coming together for me, yet every year I feel so sad on New Year's Eve; I guess it's because I see the years passing and the idea of having my own family is so far off.

In this case, we see the need to establish and start a family, but the mistake here is that the woman is the one being put in charge of solidifying the marriage. Very often, the man takes on the role of adversary and resists making the commitment. The couple has to acknowledge this situation, which is very common, and learn to balance these roles.

Any woman who works and has an independent life has to value her space and time in the same way that any man does. It is also important for the couple to realize that they're procrastinating. The decision to get married has to be a common goal for both partners and should be made with harmony and conviction.

How do we overcome these negative dynamics and maintain harmony within the rules that the couple originally agreed to? Here are some examples of how these negative situations manifest in the relationship:

- Feeling trapped, with no possibility of evolving or growing.
- Avoiding and clinging to the relationship in spite of the increasing problems, not probing deeply enough.
- Justifying physical problems so as not to confront difficulties with sex, shyness or phobias. Waiting for things to improve on their own without doing anything constructive to achieve this.
- Avoiding a confrontation with one's partner, because the partner is seen as an authoritative figure with greater power than our own.
- Fear of changing situations. A tendency to establish a model for the relationship.
- Adopting very stereotypical roles.
- Using exhaustion or feeling sleepy as an excuse to put off having sex; this is very common among well-established couples. Fatigue, even if only slight, is a fabulous resource for procrastination.
- Offering the excuse "I don't have time for that right now" in order to avoid talking about the future with one's partner.
- Opting for the role of critic and using criticism to avoid your

own unwillingness to transform negative habits within the relationship.
• Feeling bored. This is an excellent way to procrastinate and use the boredom as an excuse for not doing anything more stimulating or fun.

How do we modify these mechanisms?

• Make the decision to live moment to moment and appreciate your time together.
• Look inside yourself for the emotional resistance that forces you to put off fulfilling your own needs.
• Start writing a letter or diary in which you manifest what you desire. You will realize that you've unecessarily put things off. The simple act of becoming conscious of what you need and writing it down will help you eliminate the anxiety that the task or project brings up inside you. As a result, your partner will be happy to see you happy.
• Contact your vulnerable side, that part of you that you never listen to. Ask yourself: "What is the worst thing that could happen to me if I were to do this thing that I'm putting off right now?" Think about what motives you have for being afraid of doing something and by thinking about them, you will be able to let go.
• Give yourself a specific time period in which to complete the task that you have been putting off.
• Carefully observe your reality. Decide what you are avoiding in the present moment and begin to face your need to be happy and fulfilled. The act of postponing the task at hand is merely procrastinating in the present because of something that you fear in the future.
• Begin using your mind in a creative fashion to remedy boredom. If you are in a boring meeting, change the pace of things by asking a pertinent question, or occupy your mind with stimulating thoughts.

If your partner criticizes and limits you, and you feel you are putting off the fulfillment of your own needs, don't project your limitations onto the other person. This will allow you to move from the point of criticism to the point of action.

- Observe people or relationships that you would like to imitate. Having positive role models may help as long as you don't idolize them. Use them as a point of reference.
- Choose which emotions you want to feel in a relationship. You alone are in control of your emotions; do not allow anyone to make you feel otherwise.
- Elevate your opportunities: when you feel hurt by an onslaught of negative emotions, make a list of all the positive options that you have for reacting to the situation. This system gives you a mechanism for protecting yourself against unnecessary pain.
- Evaluate, through constant communication, the expectations that you and your partner have of one another and the relationship (harmony, passion, financial stability, social status, a family and so on).

Ivan, age twenty-eight, understands his own worth as well as that of his partner. He speaks highly of both his partner and himself and expresses pride at having chosen this person:

I've been living with my girlfriend for eleven months. We were together for two years and decided to move in together. She's incredible; she works, cooks and goes to school. You can't say too much about the person you love and still be objective, so good-bye objectivity. My girlfriend has a lot of talent for organization, and maybe for that reason, at first sight, she comes off like she's kind of serious, but she's so beautiful. I help her around the house. We do everything together. She always has a big smile on her face and a fire burning inside of her that can become aroused when you least expect it. She is spiri-

tual, ambitious and knows what she wants in life. I would go so far as to write on every street that I walk on that I love her. In short: I love her with my whole heart and soul. When are we getting married? I don't know, I tell my aunts and my mother, who are always asking. In reality, right now I just want to enjoy looking into her eyes and her smile and making love until eternity. Of course this last part is a secret.

There's not much more to say; simply enjoy love. This emotion is capable of moving mountains, and making every dream come true.

Now What?
Should We Get Married?

When it comes time to making a decision as important as whether or not to get married, it may be helpful to make a list of all those things that we gain and lose in the exchange. The fundamental thing is to do this exercise openly and consciously with your partner, attempting to be as sincere as possible with one another, keeping in mind that this self-examination of the relationship could very well change it in every sense.

Step One: From the onset, we must avoid all comparisons with other couples and myths that we have regarding marriage.

Step Two: Once we have overcome myths and comparisons with other couples, especially when it comes to the relationship that we perceive our parents to have had, we can more clearly see the things that we tend to repeat in our own relationships and not commit the same mistakes. If you've already been through a similar situation and it went badly for you, you cannot draw conclusions from that experience. Focus on your present relationship and attempt to draw all the good from your partner. When making this type of a decision, it is easy to initiate a type of reasoning known as the negative anticipator model. This mechanism consists of imagining how your life would be with that person and the possible problems that could arise.

You cannot base yourself in phrases like, "What if this and this happens?" Those things that you're thinking about have not happened, and you don't even know if they will happen, so stop imagining and focus on the present.

Step Three: The two of you can ask questions regarding what you want your life project to be together. Make a list of your negative and positive feelings regarding marriage and then compare it with your partner's list and discuss it. It's possible that you will have many things in common.

Step Four: If the negative factors seem to outweigh the positive ones, you can do an exercise to help you understand why. Try to remember situations that both of you have faced and then resolved by passing through different stages of fear or loss of courage. By reflecting upon these experiences, you will reinforce the knowledge that love is capable of positively transforming any situation.

Trust in your capacity to triumph and openly confess to your partner all of your fantasies about marriage.

Step Five: Establish rules. It's important that you consider certain factors that have to be shared: space, time, friends, money; how will you balance each of these factors? The more clearly you can discuss this beforehand, the more likely you'll achieve happiness in the future.

After this exercise you will be able to comprehend and analyze what you both really desire and whether or not you are prepared for marriage.

MYTHS ABOUT MARRIAGE

- Married people have a less fulfilling sex life than single people. This is not true: every sexual relationship depends on the personal relationship of the individuals.
- Once you get married, you lose your freedom, friends, and so on. You can actually gain new friends through marriage, as well as enjoy new and different relationships with other couples or people who enter the couple's life.
- Marriage is for the purpose of procreation. This is false. Many couples have children together without ever formalizing a marriage agreement. Conversely, many married couples remain childless.
- Marriage gives you emotional and economic security. This is only true in a healthy marriage. The high rate of divorce in today's society shows that this is not true for all.
- Marriage benefits women more than men economically. Nowadays women have a very active role in society, and a wife may have a job that provides her with as much or even more money than her husband.

It is important to remember that not only in a marriage, but in a domestic partnership of any type, there is always a period of adaptation and readjustment.

CHAPTER 6

I Love You and
I Want to Marry You

It's not just a "you" and a "me" in our project. From now on: we are a "we" with everything that we've both been carrying and loving from our past and projecting into our future; with what we're acquiring along the way, in that stream of time and space in which we live moment to moment, rising above things and enjoying every instant.

The True Meaning of Marriage

It's pretty easy to say, "I'm getting married" and even "I do," but what's difficult is learning to live as a couple. In the long run, marriage is more than just a union of two people for the purpose of creating a family; it's an irrevocable contract based on love, respect, trust and fidelity, which requires hard work on both parts. Before we get into the components of conjugal relationships, let's just say that they inevitably transition from the ecstasy of falling in love to the routine of daily life, with all its interesting, albeit less exciting, phases. The initial enthusiasm of the relationship is reduced and it lands in reality, which is nothing more than reciprocal acceptance of the virtues and flaws in each other.

This new mature love possesses the greatness of daily life, that marvelous adventure into which we may place the best of ourselves or not, depending on our degree of commitment, not only toward the other person, but toward ourselves. Living together is an excellent way of getting to know one another. It provides the satisfaction of having everything with someone who lights up your personal panorama, present and future.

Domestic love, once established, turns those initial moments in which we see life through rose-colored lenses into a rainbow of many tonalities, like life itself. Marriage can be compared to a school in which we learn the best thing in life: to give and receive love. We also learn to act with integrity, consistency and ethics. Living together requires willingness. It affirms and reinforces your love through daily conquest—tenacious, persevering and audacious. Love must be cultivated day by day; otherwise, the relationship evaporates, chills, is lost. It assumes insistence and the desire to conquer both internal and external obstacles by any means. In a domestic relationship, the exercise of our will is a decisive quality in nurturing and preserving love.

Our free will must be totally committed to love, and such a commitment of free will is possible only if one begins with sincerity. Love must be learned. The lesson requires time, but if you persevere, you learn. Isn't that how we manage all the other aspects of our lives—a business or a career, for instance? In order to make it as a doctor or a lawyer, for example, you have to study for years in a university and, even after getting a degree, you have to continue improving yourself. Much in the same manner, a person who wants to learn to love more fully should really take the opportunity to learn about the process of living together. At first we start getting to know each other and to interact, but it is only once we move in with our partner that we put the lesson into practice and continue learning every day.

Each member of the couple must face the fact that he or she is no longer living at home as a child. Now you are someone else's partner and the two of you will share your time, love, dreams, desires, money and everything else. Each one of you is an independent adult, separate from the family in which you grew up, and each must learn new ways of relating in the context of this new family. This is the most important event in your life.

There are many interesting things to share, but there are also restrictions that living as a couple imposes. For example, being in a committed relationship requires that you limit certain activities that you had freely enjoyed as a single person to make the new relationship your priority. Every member of the newly formed family has to contribute his or her own individuality, habits and way of life. These differences in lifestyle shouldn't develop into future conflicts; they should be addressed beforehand and basic agreements and compromises should be made.

There is no easy path to happiness. In marriage, love's biggest enemy is selfishness—not your partner's, but your own. Here are some tips on how to keep your marriage happy.

Learn how to agree. Lack of communication, not knowing how to resolve conflicts, not agreeing on anything, not having fun together or not supporting one another mutually—all of these can cause misunderstandings and progressive distancing between partners. Differences between the two of you will inevitably crop up. These disparities are what contain the potential richness of the relationship. Love functions when differences are respected. Diversity in the relationship should be a matter of irrevocable and nonnegotiable principle.

Practice acceptance. When I accept another person, I assume that nothing that person does, says, feels or thinks is rooted in deceit or manipulation. I give the person the benefit of the doubt and make that a matter of principle. Acceptance frees me from the need to change the other person and frees me from the risk that the person will try to convert me into something I'm not.

Be tolerant. Develop the ability to respect your partner's way of living as you do your own. We must always remember that our own beliefs and customs are no better and no worse than anybody else's. You don't have to share the same opinions in order to consider your partner's point of view to be as valid as yours. Try to put yourself in the other person's shoes and learn to enrich your relationship by embracing your differences.

Learn from your mistakes. If you make a mistake, you should accept it and try to remedy it. As a couple, you should talk about your failings with one another, share responsibilities for your mistakes and correct them, always expressing mutual support.

Take responsibility. This is the ability to take charge of your own life. This is fundamental to the existence of a relationship based on true love. You cannot make yourself responsible for another person's happiness, but you do have to be responsible for not deceiving or manipulating others.

Be free to trust. If you love something, let it go. Even within the context of a close relationship, people still need their own space. To love means to detach yourself from your own fears, prejudices, ego and conditioning. One positive thing that each of the partners can do is to repeat this affirmation: "Today I leave behind all my fears; the past has no power over me. Today is the beginning of a new life."

A key question: "Why are we together?" The answer will always be healthy and sincere, fearlessly reclaiming the sense of love that brought you together in the first place. Many couples don't want to ask themselves this because they are afraid that the answer will provoke them to feel emptiness. Yet this question is fundamental for couples who want to continuously strengthen their bond of passion. It helps the couple to assess their psychological state and unites the partners by solidifying their common goals.

Avoid threats. Threatening to end the relationship if one partner is not willing to do what the other asks is not acceptable and should not be tolerated by anyone.

Teach love. We ourselves are the ones who will teach our beloved to love us in the way that we need to be loved. When you don't feel loved as you need to be, communicate your need. Don't keep quiet. That generates resentment and nobody can read your mind.

Focus on the financial well-being of both partners. Draw up a written agreement about money and material goods. The clearer the use of mutual economic resources, the fewer problems the marriage will encounter financially. Remember that anything that elevates your partner's economic well-being will also elevate yours.

Don't go to bed without resolving your conflict. Don't take resentments to bed with you. They will only ruin your sexual relationship because sex does not always solve the problems between lovers.

Don't expect there to be a "normal" level of frequency for sex. This myth causes a lot of arguments. Every couple finds its own sexual rhythm, and that rhythm is one with which both partners are happy and satisfied without need for explanations. The theme of sexuality with all of its implications will be handled in the third part of this book.

Improve sexual communication. This is the intimate language that the couple shares through their bodies. It's a holistic form of communication that reflects the deepest desires, fears and needs of each partner, as well as the possibility of discovering different aspects of each other's personality. Sexual affection has to be considered as something that must be learned. This will be covered in the third part of the book.

INTEGRATING THE BOND

Two people who lay the foundation for a domestic partnership are in effect building a brand-new country in virgin territory. They can do this by either submitting to each other, battling for power or nourishing one another with the diversity of generating a new nation.

Each partner enters the marriage with his or her own set of baggage in which they carry their own personality, traditions and habits. But all these things have to be organized into a closet that the two of you will use at the same time and in the same space. Different sections in the closet will need to be adjusted constantly in order to accommodate your separate stuff and it eventually becomes impossible to keep the original baggage intact. What do I mean by this? I mean that the partners have to build a new space, where there will be room for those things that they must share. Later, as married life sets in, the closet begins to take a new shape, reorganizing itself, discarding the unimportant while incorporating new items. Every couple should do this after uttering the words, "I accept you for life."

Yet no matter how many things a couple may have in common, there will always be ways in which they are not alike. Were it not this way, we'd be married to our very own clone. Understanding the differences between partners helps people to mature. That is why it is so important to get to know yourself and your partner as well as possible.

Comments on Marriage

Jeannette, age thirty-one, does not attach much importance to the formality of the marriage contract, yet appreciates the public celebration of the union:

To be honest, I've had both types of experiences in my life while living with my boyfriend for four years. We had a child together, which turned into the big test for our love. Eventually, we got married for practical reasons on one hand, and out of a need for ritual on the other hand. But I can assure you that nothing's changed. In fact, I forget that I'm married sometimes. I remember it only when I have to do something that requires legal stuff, otherwise, it's just like before we got married. The bond between us is the same. The only thing I think is really nice about marriage is the idea of promising love to each other in front of your friends and family. I don't mean to imply that the ritual has to be traditional or conventional in any way, but it's good as something you do to create a special memory.

For many couples, the need to seal the relationship with some sort of ritual is important, even if it's not necessarily for religious reasons. The act of celebrating marriage is a beautiful and tender experience that we remember for all of our lives.

Edward, age thirty-four, married his high-school sweetheart and tells of his lovely experience:

In the early years of our marriage, while we were both going to college and working and we never saw each other enough, I had the false idea that a marriage could survive in the midst of that level of "nonthreatening" negligence.

Since then, however, I have learned the following truth: making a good marriage is very similar to cooking a good stew. A marriage is only as good as the ingredients that go into it. You must create time for conversation with your partner, to take a walk together, to go out to dinner on special occasions or to spend an afternoon just talking. You need to take the time to share your impressions with one another, to laugh and enjoy romantic adventures. If you don't, your marriage will not be any better than a bland stew without seasoning or flavor. When I got married, I assumed that the most important days in a marriage would be anniversaries, weddings, holidays, family reunions and the

like. But I've changed my mind, and I realize now that the most impor-
tant day in any marriage is today.

The positive thing about Edward's experience is that he learned
to appreciate the value of marriage and was able to find happiness
in the process of sharing daily life. His story illustrates the transition
that couples experience as they go from courtship to marriage, and
helps us to evaluate the factors that come into play.

Normally the early stages of living together are accompanied by
an adjustment to a new home, new lifestyle and new economic status, charging those first few moments with hope, but also with
uncertainty and fear of the unknown.

We must also remember that living together may also bring economic difficulties, lack of familial support, lack of resources and
other factors that may influence the couple's relationship. Time helps
to mature the experience, making it not any less intense, but more
objective. Many aspects of the relationship are reevaluated more
objectively than at the beginning. Many differences can influence the
functioning of a relationship once a couple moves in together, such
as work schedules, tastes, habits and economic standing.

Once partners decide to establish an adult relationship, they have
usually gotten to know the other person pretty well, things are working sexually and they love each other and enjoy good communication,
trust and respect. The understanding that harmonious cohabitation
requires acceptance of each other's personal characteristics is fundamental to a healthy and positive interaction and enables the couple to
get through tough moments without jumping to the conclusion that
the relationship isn't working.

Remember that marriage doesn't imply that all experiences must
be shared, or that partners must have the same tastes or habits.
Although it is important to have things in common and to be able
to adapt to the other person, there's no need to give up your personal
development. This is essential not only to the well-being of each
individual, but to the overall health of the relationship.

Domestic love is beautiful because it's committed. It requires an agreement, an obligation to the beloved, to be with him or her forever. There is no authentic love without a voluntary commitment through which one agrees to take care of and fulfill the needs of the beloved. Commitment, responsibility and fidelity: this is the sequence that leads to true happiness.

CHAPTER 7

I Love You—Forever?

I love you not only because you love me, but also because through our relationship I have learned to love myself and to understand my true nature.

To Love or Not to Love.
Is That the Question?

Living together is no easy feat if you consider that all of our daily problems come to rest upon this relationship. Yet in spite of all the challenges that living together may pose, I believe that there is nothing stronger than love. When two people come together in love, they generate an invincible energy field.

Since relationships are an exchange between two people, the basis for happiness lies in the ability to make that exchange a balanced and positive one. The notion of giving as much as one expects to receive will help to make your relationship a source of total satisfaction.

My own experience has taught me that being committed to a balanced domestic relationship offers the opportunity to really grow as a human being, on every level and in the deepest sense. My husband and I had some wonderfully intimate experiences, but the domestic relationship between us was somewhat difficult for me in the beginning. I had to make many adjustments, especially during our first two years together, because I had moved to a new country and transformed my entire life to be with him.

Love After "I Love You"

Across a vast distance,
A distance insurmountable just a hundred years past
Two people connected
Through a wire
Like a nerve
That stretches the brain beyond
Beyond where eye can see
Or ear hear
Or skin touch
Forming a pool of commonality among that which is most
    uncommon
Or rather finding the commonality that exists everywhere
Covered by culture and tradition
Masked by language
Obscured by words, gestures
Buried in unfamiliar symbols
Still the most common remains.
But this most common
This thread that runs through everything
Connects everything
Joins everything
Sweetens everything
Is not so common after all
It is in fact, the rarest of gifts
That keeps its rareness even when it is everywhere
It is love.
Love makes the wire
Moves the hand
Fires the synapse and
Stretches the reach of consciousness

Way beyond the tiny borders of its body
Reaching to the other side of the world to capture and win the heart
    of its beloved.
Greg (your husband)

My husband, Greg, and I met on the Internet. We had a virtual relationship for several months until finally we met and never parted again. It's a very romantic story for another book, but I will share some of the details so that you may get to know me better.

Greg lived in New York while I lived in Buenos Aires. We had different life experiences, different cultures. Nonetheless, we found in one another that special spiritual connection that is strong enough, even today, to nourish a beautiful relationship.

We both constantly have the sensation that we are fused together spiritually. Two become one and are joined in a single breath, a single flame, a shared heart.

Greg and I have always joked about how it seemed as if it took a century to find each other. Possibly we were waiting for the age of technology. Without the virtual revolution, it would have been impossible for two people to come together who lived many miles apart and in completely different universes.

My husband and I practice visualization techniques and we each guide the other in getting to know ourselves better, both as individuals and as a couple. These exercises help us tremendously to grow and to expand our love. I advise all of my readers to practice the exercises offered throughout this book, preferably with your partner.

Living Together Tests Love

When I was writing this section of the book, I kept dreaming that I had to take some tests but couldn't take them because I was using a notebook and not a computer, so I wasn't able to turn in the tests on time. In reality, I never write in notebooks or on paper because my handwriting is too hard to decipher, so much so that even I can't read it sometimes. I like to write on any computer I can find, and gave up paper seventeen years ago when I last wrote poetry.

The dream conveyed to me that life as a couple is like a permanent test of our doubts, our self-questioning, our insecurities and desires, but it is also a celebration of freedom. To love somebody else you must love yourself first so that you can accept the other person with all of his or her flaws and virtues.

Living together brings about a whole new set of experiences. Sometimes conflicts crop up, along with fears, insecurity and other problems. This doesn't necessarily occur only when a couple lives together. It can also happen in any relationship characterized by a certain degree of commitment. It also happens around the same time that we stop seeing things through rose-colored glasses. By this point we're emotionally invested enough to continue with the relationship. It doesn't seem like an option to pack our bags and head for the nearest hotel.

At this stage, expectations increase in both parties and each comes to expect the other to be perfect. Each one carries the belief that the relationship wasn't supposed to cause anyone any problems because when we give our love, in exchange, we demand perfection from the other person without realizing that we ourselves aren't perfect.

This is a basic issue in a relationship. It's something we just don't think about, however, because in spite of being able to say "I love you," very few people are actually able to see things from the other's perspective. As I explained in the early chapters of this book, every relationship is a mirror. As in the famous fairy tale "Beauty and the Beast," you are actually expecting to see "beauty" in your mirror or reflection (your partner).

Of course it's not fair for you to demand that your partner provide you with beauty and perfection in exchange for your love, especially when you yourself are not conscious of the parts of yourself that are irrational, negative or banal. But the fun part is (though it might be something to cry about) the fact that the other person is also expecting to see only beauty and perfection in you! Therefore, the million-dollar question is: Who's the monster? My answer is: the monster is actually a projection of ourselves.

As a result, we begin to see the marriage, commitment or relationship as horrific. So if the love that starts out pure and sweet ends up becoming a monster, why bother falling in love? On the other hand, when we take charge of the mirror and accept the other person as he or she is, we learn to accept ourselves. We seek out ways to improve ourselves as human beings, without resorting to extreme polarities such as beautiful and horrible, good and evil, conflict and harmony. We can then participate in a mature relationship that offers clarity and the possibility of being vulnerable, certainly a fertile and powerful experience.

Every healthy relationship between lovers is vulnerable to change, crisis, transformation, evolution and improvement. In spite of the promises that are made and the papers that are signed, nothing can guarantee that the passion will survive the implacable test of time. Nonetheless, one can affirm that thanks to acceptance, the relationship is capable of growing and maturing. Once the initial passionate phase is over, and the relationship continues despite this, people recover their true personalities and traces of habitual patterns begin to emerge, but not always to the partner's satisfaction. Most of us are aware that there is some part of our personality that requires some level of modification, but we don't necessarily like the idea.

That is precisely the challenge of being in a couple. Whether a relationship lasts a day or a lifetime, it teaches us about ourselves, and allows us to learn from our greatest teachers in life: those who *love* us, and who really, really know us.

Falling Out of Love

Caroline, age thirty-five, was in love when she got married, but perhaps she really didn't know her husband well enough. After working with her inner self, she realized that her situation was not likely to improve unless she and her husband worked on it. Her experience is as follows:

Just like that, overnight, everything changed. I thought I was sleeping with a stranger, someone I had never met. G and I had been living together for four or five years and we had been married for two. We decided to go see a therapist, since we weren't listening to each other, we didn't understand each other and it seemed like each of us was speaking a different language. We'd say really senseless things, and we avoided sex, using all kinds of excuses. I noticed that sometimes he'd be sweet and tender like he was at the beginning of the relationship, but that would disappear pretty quickly. It seemed like we were together just out of habit, simply out of inertia. We no longer shared anything, not even the dreams we had together.

I was pretty sad about going from being in love to being out of love in such a short time. We didn't know why. We needed help, we told ourselves. Luckily, we started working on the inner couple and began to understand more about ourselves and about how to reconcile with love. As if by magic, we started kissing again and making love, but more important, what we got back was the desire and the joy of being together.

Feelings are not just simple emotions that happen without rhyme or reason. Feelings are reactions that we choose or that arise because of our personality and its patterns of conditioning.

In Caroline's case, she and her husband worked with the inner couple, a subject I will address in the next chapter. She understood clearly that a relationship, if not properly cared for, will be plagued by disappointment, boredom and frustration.

She was advised by her therapist that they participate in enjoyable activities together, thus making the relationship more satisfying and stable. Having fun together is one more way to help prevent the relationship from being damaged by daily challenges.

Yet while it's true that a couple needs to spend time together, every adult needs to spend time alone as well. Each partner needs time to feel relaxed and free, as this time apart ultimately nurtures the relationship. And here lies one of the most common problems among couples: some people don't understand that their partner desires to be alone at times.

CHAPTER 8

I Love You Because
You're My Ideal Mate

*Someone loves you for what you are, adores the way you make
him or her feel and is affected by everything you do, think
or feel.*
Someone is pleased to have you as a friend, lover and partner.
*Someone has stayed up all night thinking about you and hoping
that you'll understand him or her.*
*Someone misses your help and wants to find you to get to know
you better.*
*Someone has confidence in you, knows what you're worth and
needs your love and your support.* That someone is you.

The Inner Couple

Every individual has masculine and feminine qualities, though they
may not realize it. All of us carry masculine and feminine energy
and they make up the "inner couple." This inner couple may have
either a positive or a negative relationship. When the relationship
is conflictive, it leaks out into the person's relationship with his or
her partner becuase the inner drama is projected onto the outer
world.

Feminine energy is intuitive, deep, wise and guides all of us from within. Our female energy speaks to us through inner impulses, our most visceral aspects, or through our intuition. When we're not sufficiently in touch with our feminine energy, it reveals messages to us through dreams as well as emotional changes.

The inner masculine energy, on the other hand, manifests in the outer world through our daily activities, such as work and sports.

A well-balanced human being is both active and flexible, rational and intuitive, strong and tender, aggressive and receptive. When these masculine and feminine qualities are present in proportion to one another, they lead to emotional equilibrium and to healthy and loving relationships with our partner. Falling in love is one example of how we project our masculine or feminine part onto the image of the ideal man or woman.

In order to understand the totality that we are as beings, beyond polarities, we must understand these two realms of our reality, because these energies play an important part in relationships. The result of this inner relationship is that when projected onto the outside world, it attracts our actual love partners.

The masculine and feminine reside inside each of us like a seed—it's the core of our very existence. Once you realize that your mate lives inside of you, you feel secure, protected and sure of yourself and your partner, because you know that you can change your world from the inside out. It's not about changing the other person—it's about changing yourself. This way you're not searching for that person who is right, your perfect other. You already know that the key to happiness is inside you and that it all depends on your own level of awareness.

By relating to our polar energies—feminine and masculine—our relationship to the other person will change radically: it will become much simpler. Many of the different psychological problems that affect our relationships with the opposite sex (and this usually includes quite a few problems) will automatically disappear.

How Do We Recognize the Masculine and Feminine Energy in Ourselves?

There is no night without day, no woman without man, no earth without sky. The vital movement of the creation of everything that exists is an exchange between the complementary feminine and masculine forces.

Inside every male human being there is a vital feminine force, represented at the mental level as an inner woman. Inside of every woman there is a mental representation of masculine energy or an inner man. These polar images contain qualities and flaws that most people aren't aware of because they function at an unconscious level; hence, that image is projected onto our partner and others that we may relate to.

According to Jungian and Gestalt psychologists, and ancient philosophers like the Taoists, the energy that represents the masculine force is activity, the day, dryness, the sun, fire and aggression (though I note that aggression in its balanced and correct state is a positive vital instinct, because it helps us defend ourselves). The feminine energy is represented by passivity, night, humidity, cold, water and the moon.

Discovering her masculine polarity actually helps a woman's femininity to flourish. On the other hand, when a man is out of touch with his feminine polarity, his masculinity will have a very mental, rational tendency, demonstrating denial of his own sensitivity and making him far more fragile than his macho attitude might imply.

If we consider that inside of every man and woman there is a masculine and a feminine part, the first task required to make a relationship work is for partners to develop both parts until they can each celebrate a true inner marriage. If a man doesn't value his intuitive, vulnerable and sensitive side, he will always project it onto his partner. He may place excessive demands on her or crush her with lack of appreciation. A woman who isn't connected to her masculine energy doesn't value and develop her capacity to reason or her sense of power, success or self-sustenance in the world. She may either become dependent upon her partner or resent him for her own apathy and inertia; she may not trust her ability to make decisions, and may resort to playing the role of victim.

A man who is not in touch with his masculine energy may become too passive sexually and in his interpersonal relationships, and he may tend to relinquish the power he has over his own life to others. A woman who has not developed her feminine side may be excessively competitive or extremely dominant in sex.

It also happens sometimes that the woman's masculine aspect may compete with the man or crush his feminine side. Or the man's feminine side becomes jealous of the woman's, or his masculine side feels humiliated because she wants to make the decisions at home. Until we become aware of this power exchange, negative situations may multiply infinitely.

OBJECTIVES OF THE INNER COUPLE

Once you connect to your true self, you will be able to feel how the entire universe is created and expanded inside of you and assists your growth on every level. Explore your unconscious by doing the exercises in the next section. Don't spare any effort in surrendering to this task. Follow the transformations that arise from these apparently spontaneous fantasies. These images are actually deep realities that you are revealing to yourself for the benefit of your own higher consciousness and sense of abundance. Stay constantly alert and be careful as you perform each of these exercises. It's best to write them in a notebook so that you can see how they develop and change. Don't focus too much on what happens in your relationships when you begin working. Each situation that comes up can be a test of your work or a confirmation of your achievements. Just take each external element as part of the process—all you need to do is deepen your inner task. Below I list the objectives of the visualization exercises:

- Become aware of our feminine and masculine aspects and their positive functions.
- Unblock our emotional and mental obstacles.
- Perceive the expansion of our own potential.
- Experience our own energy in action.
- Apply what we have experienced and learned through techniques.
- Find and recognize your inner mate.
- Project your external partner from a position of true inner harmony.

Visualization of the Inner Couple: Feminine and Masculine Energies

If you can relax and listen to the beating of your heart, there you will find the nucleus and essence of totality.

Visualization is a technique that is used for much more than just mental relaxation. We attempt to use our imagination to create images that may or may not be related to our subconscious, depending on the goal that we are pursuing. This technique is used widely in psychotherapy, in meditation and in yoga.

The benefits that are obtained through this technique are as follows:

- Increasing the degree of perception and true consciousness of all of our feelings and emotions.
- Developing the mental potential that is so rarely acknowledged and used.

- Opening new energetic channels that guide us (with practice).
- The expansion of innate faculties such as intuition and inner power.
- In short, we become better able to perceive our own reality, not only in the bodily sense but also on the spiritual and mental levels.

This technique is comprised of some simple and very precise exercises; it takes a total of about fifteen to twenty minutes to develop. The prior relaxation takes about ten minutes, but after repeated practice, one reaches a deeper state of relaxation more quickly.

We sometimes don't realize the importance of doing and experiencing these exercises. Now, make the decision to change your relationships by way of the internal work that is offered below.

The first thing is relaxation. This is of vital importance since it allows us to program our minds in a positive way and thus initiate the path of inner exploration. To relax means to release tension from every muscle in the physical body so that energy can flow freely. We feel much lighter, and can even free ourselves from the afflictions of our physical bodies.

The Place: Choose a quiet room where nobody can interrupt you for at least half an hour. This practice can be carried out with friends or with your partner—it's not necessary to do it alone—but there shouldn't be anyone in the room who is not assisting in your internal work.

Light some candles or use very dim light. If you wish, select some tranquil music to help you concentrate. Wear comfortable clothing and take off your watch. You may lie down on the floor, preferably on a rug, sheet or mat, or relax in a comfortable chair. Your arms should not be crossed, but resting at either side of your body. It's best if the palms of your hands are facing upward.

The Positions: There are two ideal positions that should be used to achieve an adequate level of relaxation:

1. Lying down face up with your back straight, your feet slightly apart, your arms extended alongside your body and the palms of your hands facing upward.
2. Sitting comfortably on a pillow or in a chair, with your spine straight and your feet crossed comfortably in front of you.

In either position you should wear clothing that is loose, that does not pinch or bind and is not cumbersome.

Breathing and relaxing the muscles: Breathe as deeply as you can three times. Now focus your attention on your feet. Take your time to feel them. Imagine how much they weigh and then relax; feel the weight, then relax. Keep bringing your attention upward toward your tibia (shin bone), calves and knees.

Don't rush: Feel yourself entering an increasingly deeper state of calm. Continue moving up your body bringing your energy toward your thighs, genitals, buttocks and waist, relaxing them more and more. Keep your breathing calm and tranquil.

Continue moving your relaxation upward through your body: Move the energy up through your abdomen, chest, back, shoulders, arms and hands. Feel how each area of your body expands and relaxes more and more. Keep moving upward, bringing your attention now toward your neck, and focus your attention on this area, which is very easily blocked by daily stress. Continue to the muscles in your face, your scalp and finally to your mind. Try to keep your mind blank, and continue in this state before going on to the next step.

Visualization and mental relaxation: Try to eliminate all thoughts from your mind, but without making a lot of effort. Everything has to happen naturally. Now, visualize a beloved place in nature, where you would love to be at this very moment. Here are some examples (you choose the location that you want): a lake, mountains, the forest, countryside, desert, beach or sky.

Breathe deeply: You can keep your eyes open or closed at first, until you acquire a sense of security and experience in meditation. After that, it will become easier to keep your eyes closed through the whole exercise. Once you find yourself in that beloved place, try to put yourself entirely in that space. Feel the temperature of the place you've chosen, connect with the feelings that it brings you. If there are people that you love or strangers there, notice your reaction to them. Observe the nature of the place, its plants, flowers, earth, animals, water and so on. Accept all the ideas and visions that come to your mind. Once you are totally relaxed, you are ready for the next step.

Visualizing the Inner Masculine Energy in Both Sexes

I am the awareness of man that exists with me and inside of me
And of woman who resides inside of me.

Have you ever asked yourself why you always choose a partner with certain characteristics that are similar to your last partner when you actually desire something different? In this exercise, which is the same for both men and women, you will understand why this happens. You will be able to abandon the negative relationships that you had in the past, and erase the unpleasant memories they've left. You will be free to concentrate your energy on renewing your current relationship through more creative and promising exchanges. Every new seed that grows from this process will generate moments of happiness between you and your partner.

As stated earlier, this exercise has positive benefits for both sexes. The objective is for you to know yourself, explore and deepen your vital potency by your own action, by means of your own capacity to generate energy and enthusiasm, and to stimulate your inner power in its totality. If you want to prepare for physical or mental activity, carry out this visualization and you will feel as though your creative energy is infinite and whole.

Continue in your state of relaxation. Visualize yourself walking through a fertile meadow. Don't stop to look behind you. Feel how hundreds of seeds emerge and escape from the palms of your hands. As they drop, they grow into infinitely beautiful trees of different colors and shapes, with different fruits and flowers. Visualize this magical change that is produced by your creativity.

Exploring Your Instinctive Impulses

We all have impulses and emotions that are destructive in our relations. It's part of our humanness. This exercise will help you better understand the pure, primal, less rational masculine energy. This visualization serves the purpose of exploring our positive instincts, not only in order to ensure our survival but to strengthen our connection to pure passion and potency in our sexual and emotional relationships. This following exercise, as all of those explained in this text, is for both sexes.

Imagine a wild, black horse galloping through an immense pasture. This wild animal is like a savage beast that has never been mounted or ridden. Imagine that this horse represents your impulses, which sometimes seem uncontrollable to yourself and to others. Now think about how you can tame this wild creature. Imagine what this horse might need. Perhaps it has never been caressed, never been gazed upon with love. Try to think of ways to make the animal your friend. Approach it little by little. Pet it and show it affection. Slowly but surely, it starts becoming domesticated. It approaches you and somehow lets you know that you can ride through the meadow on its back. As you ride, you see the orange rays of the sun on the horizon, and before you know it, you find yourself rising as the horse begins to change color. It's becoming a white horse that flies across the universe toward the sun. You can see your thoughts and emotions light up as you soar through the heavens, and you become aware of your impulses. The sun represents your consciousness, and the flight on the white horse is a symbol of your mind's ability to tame your impulses and emotions.

By repeating this visualization exercise several times a month, you will become much more conscious of your sexual energy. This will help you to identify your true desires by helping you to distinguish them from negative impulses. This exercise also helps you understand your inner self and will also give you the ability to understand the needs of others and offer compassion.

Deepening the Inner Feminine Energy in Both Sexes

Feminine energy is creative, passive, and attempts to conform, understand and integrate the needs of everyone. It feels compassion for all beings and turns conflict into harmony. Feminine energy has many different aspects and visual representations, as might a goddess or a flower. See yourself as an open flower—feel all of the beauty that you radiate, the fragrance that you exude, the way the sun makes your energy expand. Feel yourself opening more and more and experience how you are connected to all of creation.

The Goddess of Love and How to Recognize Your Emotions

Place before you the image of an archetypal figure, such as the statue of the Virgin Mother, a goddess or an image of any woman (it's best if you do not associate her with anyone in particular) who radiates compassion and tranquillity. Feel the way in which she gives you all of her love, comforts you and calms all your anxiety. She takes you by the hand and leads you to the edge of a lake whose waters are dark and turbulent. She says to you: "These are your emotions." You sit beside the water's edge and suddenly a beautiful maiden appears from within the lake, where she lives. She takes a chalice in her hand and says, "Drink from this water, this pure and fresh water that lives inside your own heart. It is filled with wisdom; drink from it."

You drink the water that she offers you and at once you feel the water purifying your emotions. The lake symbolizes your primary emotions, those that originate in your childhood and develop in your adult life. The woman in the lake represents your consciousness. By drinking the water you realize that you can control your emotions and can actually be nourished by them. You may feel that you can survive purely on this source of love that's constantly flowing inside you; hence you will realize that you can take care of yourself whenever you need to, especially in the relationship with your partner.

Expressing Tenderness

Sometimes people aren't affectionate or tender because they feel negative emotions that block their ability to express love. This exercise will help you to release the feelings that nurture tenderness and affection. The idea is for the person to understand and peel back his feelings of anger, thus allowing him to be more in touch with his more tender side. Close your eyes slowly and relax, using the method of relaxation described earlier. Allow your mind to see your and others' thoughts of violence and unloving behaviors that bother you. Remember concrete situations in which you weren't able to control your own emotions and in which feelings of violence and aggression dominated your entire being and created conflicts between yourself and your loved ones.

Now try to relax and visualize a pure and warm light that embraces you with the greatest tenderness, dissolving all the aggression that exists within you. Visualize how that crystalline light transforms your heart into something pure and loving, allowing the force of its tenderness to empower you.

Improving Relationships

This exercise will help you to resolve conflicts from the past. Since love transcends time and space, practice this whenever you feel that your heart is blocked by negative emotions from the past.

Carry out the relaxation exercise. Once you achieve your state of inner calm, visualize and remember those moments during which you've had problems or conflicts with your partner, moments during which you felt dissatisfied, or simply a moment that you would like to change. Instead of looking at the past, look at the future, as a director would making a new film. Correct that situation with a different script and observe the true desire, feelings and thoughts that you want to manifest in each instance. Create a happy ending for each scene and continue confirming that the film is now correctly remade. Now you can go on with your life, surrender all regret and open your heart every day increasingly to total happiness. Affirm within yourself that from now on, your decisions will be genuinely balanced and that you are no longer afraid of making mistakes. Trust in yourself.

As we connect with our inner feelings with these exercises, we begin to see and recognize our true identity. Through this process, we can modify our external circumstances by realizing that they originate inside us.

Objective reality is what exists in our external environment: the conditions and stimuli that we receive through our senses. Subjective reality is that which exists solely inside of us. The most important thing to note is that subjective reality is what governs our behavior. Once we become aware of that subjective reality, the brain programs a psychological response to that information. According to the information that it receives, the brain sets forth a certain code of behavior, and our behavior dictates what we achieve in life.

In this chapter I've shown that people possess what they need to bring about change in their lives. You really can change what you want to change, and everything in life can be improved.

By learning to tap into our inner source, we can project an external reality filled with happiness, satisfaction and love; by sharing this reality with others, we create a unique and wondrous universe.

CHAPTER 9

I Love You and I Am Willing to Transform My Fears

Fear creates distrust and provokes us to feel sorry for ourselves.

Whenever a person feels fear, he or she will create enemies where they did not exist. This is how fear keeps refueling itself. If there actually is an enemy somewhere, the very suspicion that one is in danger provokes further terror.

The reality is that we cannot avoid the fact that fears come up, that you can face them, and that you can actually become their friend.

Losing Love: Fear and Its Negative Zones

As mentioned earlier in this book, I receive thousands of questions on my website from different countries, yet they all possess similar themes of lost love, jealousy, abandonment, anguish and anxiety. Toxic emotions such as pain, guilt, shame, fear and deception accumulate in the soul. In this chapter we will explore the causes of toxic emotions, their functioning mechanisms and how you can eliminate them.

When we mention the opposite of love, people think of hate. On the other hand, one thing I am certain of is this: the only enemy of love is fear.

As young children we are trained to deny or control fear, rather than to try to understand it as a natural emotion. Society programs us to not feel fear, yet there is nothing less human than the inability to feel fear. To deny fear is to provoke toxic and negative emotions that create problems in our relationships. The important thing is that we learn to befriend our own fear. The best approach is to put the emotion in front of you, get to know it, accept it, understand it and finally become friends with the ghost that your mind created.

This is no outside enemy. It is only the negative energy that we carry inside of ourselves. The mind knows how to set traps using fear. The mind knows how to paralyze you. Don't feed your mind with ideas such as "I'd like to be something but I can't be that," "I want something but my fate limits me from having it," or "I need to do something, but I have some kind of bad karma," or anything of the sort.

Eliminate the Fear of Love
from Your Mind

The root of fear lies in the conviction that things exist outside of us and have nothing to do with our minds. Once we understand that every phenomenon is a projection of the mind, such as objects in a dream, all of our fears and problems disappear.

Note that the mind works on two fundamental principles:

1. We can only think about one thing at a time.
2. When we concentrate on a thought, the thought becomes reality because our body transforms it into action.

This is why it helps to do this exercise when irrational thoughts crop up inside of you. Use this technique as you would when something goes wrong with your computer: erase, delete and start over.

For example: "I'm sure my husband will be in a bad mood today and we'll probably argue about . . ." Think instead at that moment: "I'm eliminating these negative thoughts that are programming my day, my relationships and/or my work, creating a negative situation." In general, these negative ideas create the situation to confirm what our mind has anticipated. That is why we should wipe out these negative programs that were generated by our minds for no logical reason.

There are also exercises to wipe out these ideas by their roots. Thoughts act much as a closed-circuit system. When you eliminate that circle of thoughts, the mind creates new possibilities. You should repeat the words "I am eliminating this negative thought" until you manage to break the mental circle. It can take about two minutes. If you practice this exercise every time a toxic or negative thought creeps into your mind, you will break the negative cycle of that thought. You will then begin to hear your ideas outside of irrational emotions. Your mind will be free of concepts that nag you and prevent you from growing within your relationships.

Fatal Attraction: Anxiety and Fear

Anxiety and fear are a duo that exists throughout our lives. The function of fear is to prepare and protect us from genuine danger. When the danger is not concrete, we feel anxiety, a sensation of being threatened by a situation that may in fact be irrational. Anxiety can be experienced in different ways—those butterflies in your tummy that you feel before a first date; the muscular tension you may feel on a special occasion; your heart beating quickly when you're about to try something new. More subtle physical signs can be dryness in the throat or mouth, or dilation of the pupils. Anxiety may be provoked by a number of factors:

- Lack of self-confidence
- Anticipation of failure
- Excessively high expectations

- Worrying without reason
- Suspicion
- A tendency to shut off or to isolate ourselves
- Anger
- Pessimism
- Exaggerated self-criticism
- A tendency to concentrate on the negative
- Emotional instability
- Self-pity
- Feelings of guilt, confusion or failure

The positive thing we should know about anxiety is that it can incite us to action.

What Happens When Anxiety and Fear Come Together?

Fear always implies the presence of some sort of danger, be it real or imagined. Anxiety may be the presence of an idea or feeling that we need to express. But for some reason, we are not completely sure about the idea or we feel that there is nothing we can do in light of the situation. Fear prevents us from facing our anxiety. Fear also does not allow love to flow, either toward others or toward ourselves. The very fear of not being loved, accepted, taken care of and so forth also generates anxiety. In turn, these mechanisms create a vicious cycle.

Sometimes we seek or attract relationships with people who have prior commitments. By knowing ahead of time that there's no way a relationship will work out, the mind is able to free itself from anxiety. These people, as if by fatal attraction, seek impossible relationships. How do you stop that mechanism?

Fear manifests as a mental voice that says to us: "Don't do it: it's dangerous, you can't do it." At that very moment, the resources that we have available to confront the situation are limited. We all know this sensation; it paralyzes us completely. In order to understand and free yourself from the negative mechanisms that feed your toxic emotions and fear, you can carry out the following internal work.

Love's Kingdom

Once we become conscious of our inner world, we begin to know our own emotional mechanisms and learn to modify those that we want to change. Return to your state of visualization and relaxation. You may carry out this exercise while either sitting or lying down. Breathe slowly through your nose and mouth, regulating your breathing until you reach a point where you've totally calmed your mind. Feel your body relaxing, especially your face and neck. Keep your eyes closed. To unblock your energy and to use your entire mental resources in a positive way, visualize a very calm, transparent lake; you begin to float and you relax your entire body, liberating your mind. You feel your mind emitting images and freeing them. Contained inside each image is a little story; allow them to free themselves so that you will not be loaded down with ideas. Now visualize yourself and try to feel your body in that place as though you were a king or queen who rules over a great kingdom. This empire is your very own universe, your life, your world and the manner in which you face relationships.

Now set forth the laws of your kingdom as though you were writing the constitution that will govern your life and your relationship. Make each law as clear as possible; keep a piece of paper close by so that you can actually write down the laws once you finish doing the meditation.

Plan how you will rule your kingdom with wisdom, power and love; visualize peace and prosperity across the land. As outlined in the previous chapter, your subjective reality will trigger new behaviors in your life. As you change, the people around you will also change their behavior. This exercise is very powerful because it helps you to understand that you will attract to your life all that you wish. Revise your list of laws periodically and try to be liberal and merciful with yourself. Fear will begin to dissipate from your life. Love will reign over each day and over each part of you.

The mind undergoes constant dialogue with itself about things that surround us, our lives, feelings, concepts, self-image and so forth. Sometimes, because of traumatic experiences, personal or social pressures, this dialogue doesn't help us to live our lives to the fullest. That's when we realize that when faced with similar situations our preconceived notions and prejudices keep us from behaving as we'd like to, causing unfavorable outcomes. Not surprisingly, similar behaviors produce similar results. The purpose of the exercises outlined in this book is to influence that mental dialogue in a positive manner. This change will assist you in wiping out all the fears that act as direct enemies of love.

Open Your Heart without Fear

Living as a couple is an art. It doesn't only imply the intention to formalize a relationship, but also the willingness to work as a team to stay together through thick and thin.

It is, very simply, something that two humans are willing to embark on together as a lifelong project to make their existence more complete.

If we can look with affection upon those parts of our daily lives that don't seem too fulfilling, if we can accept them, communicate whatever we don't like about them, and try to help the other person to improve, only then will true love grow unconditionally. Here are some tips that never fail:

1. Let what the other person says penetrate your mind and heart, without any conditioning or prejudice, pay attention to what the other person needs, what your partner is asking for.
2. Just listen. Before you begin to defend, before you begin to justify, think "I don't know." Maybe that's it: I *don't* know. Maybe it's just my ego poking its head and being defensive right now.

Then wait, reflect in silence. Don't answer, don't respond automatically. Leave a space of silence before speaking.

You'll notice that something's happening, something is changing. The automatic mechanisms no longer have any power over you. You're listening, trusting and loving. You no longer fear; there's nothing or anyone from which to defend yourself. Your partner is part of you.

❧

CHAPTER 10

I Love You and I Don't Want to Argue with You

How often do you argue with your partner? Once a day, twice a week, ten times a month, twelve times a year? If you answered the latter, you are among life's most fortunate human beings.

Arguments Kill Relationships

Arguments are stressful, toxic and draining. And generally, they don't lead to any solutions. Although, arguments are healthy when they focus on one particular topic. Arguments can also be constructive when the couple decides to air out their emotions coherently or clear up some past confusion. This can alleviate accumulated misunderstandings. Usually during a positive argument, the couple comes up with some sort of resolution for the conflict. This may lead to one or both partners modifying their behavior, and this is the way in which arguments can help a relationship to grow. Unfortunately, however, the most common arguments are those that provoke more conflict in the relationship, are not at all "healthy" and are characterized primarily by irrational discussions that don't lead to any solutions.

Before entering into any argument, though sometimes our impulses don't allow us to think clearly at that moment, the ideal thing would be to ask yourself: Is this really worth arguing about? In other words, is it worth sacrificing the peace that is reigning between us to bring up this discussion right now? If the subject is trite, you'd do best to keep the peace and avoid the confrontation. If, on the other hand, the subject is really important to the overall well-being of the family or the relationship, then you must decide how to best approach the subject to avoid hurting your partner or damaging your relationship.

It may not be worthwhile to have an argument if your partner

- wears something that you don't like. Instead, carefully tell him or her that you really prefer another outfit.
- gives you the same thing for your birthday as last year. Laugh it off and remind him or her. Perhaps your partner hadn't realized it. Later, you can go and exchange the gift for something else.
- calls you "pumpkin" in front of your friends. Whisper in his or her ear that you'd really rather hear that kind of talk only in private.
- burns your dinner. Laugh it off and offer another solution.
- buys him- or herself something expensive as a personal treat. Congratulate your partner and admit that everybody needs a perk once in a while.
- needs to call his or her mother every day. If you really cannot stand to listen to their conversation, lock yourself in your bedroom and turn the music up.
- gets together once a week with friends. Follow his or her example and do it yourself. It's great for the relationship to get some air.

Below is a list of situations which may warrant a more heated exchange. You may need to have a serious discussion if your partner

- treats you badly or is abusive.
- tries to seduce someone else in front of you.

- treats your children in a way that you don't like.
- doesn't fulfill parental responsibilities.
- never lets you know about being home late.
- doesn't sleep at home.
- verbally harasses you.
- is irresponsible about work and you have to carry all the financial weight.

These are only a few examples. Obviously, the list is endless. The purpose of naming these things is to realize that there are instances that justify an argument, while others don't. If you must argue, do it with respect and try not to lose your cool. Think of the well-being of your relationship as well as your own well-being.

Arguments and fights follow the snowball effect: they start out small, as a meaningless thing, and grow until they become a disaster. Arguments are usually produced by the tendency to try to convince the other person to see things from our point of view. In any argument, we always believe that we are the one who is correct. Therefore, we don't listen to the other person's arguments, and we enter into a struggle. If one does listen, it is only to try to outdo the person's reasoning because our own is much stronger, more justifiable and certainly more factual.

- What do you feel when you see someone arguing or fighting?
- What is the first thing you think?
- Do you think that either of you wants to win the argument or is trying to dominate the other person?
- Are you arguing over jealousy or power?

You are justifying yourself as you read these words, aren't you? The best thing for you to do is answer truthfully in order to improve communication and reach a resolution.

MOTIVES THAT LEAD TO ARGUMENTS

Generally, arguments are generated by automatic thoughts that don't allow us to listen to the other person. They also do not give us space to register our own feelings and thoughts.

Automatic thoughts are like an inner monologue or dialogue with our inner selves on a mental level. This dialogue is expressed as thoughts or images that are related to intense emotional states such as anxiety, depression, anger or euphoria. Often they provide us with a false image or interpretation of things and events. In general, everything that you say or think is based on emotional distortions. Those automatic thoughts are different from the reflective thoughts we use to analyze problems. Those thoughts are clear thoughts.

Automatic thoughts show up in the mind as key phrases that provoke us:

"I'm sure she'll want to bring that up again."

"Everything makes him feel bad. What will he attack me with today?"

"What's wrong with this picture? What did I do wrong?"

Automatic thoughts are involuntary. These are usually inner dialogues produced by fear, lack of trust, low self-esteem and guilt. These reactions are learned during infancy as a momentary reflection of attitudes and beliefs, generally originating at home, at school and as a product of other social influences. During this period of growth, the person still has not fully developed the capacity for analysis. These reactions are assimilated into part of a person's personality. They accumulate in the memory waiting to be triggered by situations involving a strong emotional charge. During this moment, when the person feels incapable of solving or confronting a particular issue, these thoughts trigger automatically.

More Confessions

This is what happens to those who don't argue but also don't attempt to communicate:

Patricia and Joe have been married for nine years. They love and respect each other, and they appear to be a very happy couple. But we know that appearances can be misleading, and both partners admit that for some time now, everything seems to have changed between them. They get along very well on a day-to-day basis, and in fact, they don't argue anymore, much less fight. They seem to always agree on everything and they actually seem more like best friends than a couple.

Patricia, age thirty-eight: *We don't fight; in reality, we hardly talk. Before, what I liked most about him was his sense of humor and his capacity to surprise me constantly with little things that filled our relationship with passion. Now I feel that our lives are so dull that we've lost our essence.*

Joe, age thirty-nine: *Patricia was extremely sexy when I met her. She was always dressed to kill and that was very important to our relationship. Now it seems that she's not like she used to be. She doesn't care about those little details anymore, and our sex life has become mechanical and almost nonexistent. What's most depressing is the absence of romance and passion that has taken over the relationship for a long time now.*

Patricia and Joe's story is also that of thousands of couples who have fallen into a routine relationship but who still have time to reconstruct the base that initially brought them together, before romance totally disappears. "We used to argue a lot, but now we hold back," says Joe. Not arguing and not reaching a logical agreement is worse. Silence for fear of an explosion does just as much to ruin a relationship as does constant bickering.

In a romantic partnership, arguments are a natural occurrence. Sometimes we develop new habits and new differences surface. It is important that our partners know and understand this. But if we don't attempt to minimize arguments, arguing can become a habit—a threatening element that works against the climate of tranquillity and understanding required for a relationship's healthy development. It's devastating when a couple cannot communicate their feelings, and when each disagreement becomes increasingly more violent and the relationship disintegrates even further:

Albert, age thirty-six, was married and very much in love with his wife, yet they fell into a negative pattern of continuous arguing. They didn't realize how much damage these arguments did to their relationship. Now, feeling devastated over the end of his marriage, Albert explains:

She finally left, took her things and, after five years of marriage, she's gone. Her motives? Does anybody know why problems and domestic disputes begin? They wander through the past, the present and the future. Recriminations that have been hidden inside the soul of each person surface violently and are spurted out with no more filter than a mind that seeks to make those words as sharp and cutting as possible.

It's unbelievable that two people who loved one another so deeply could end up with what seemed like so much hatred between them, and conveniently fed this hatred in one another for years. I mean, it's true that there were a lot of things that finally made me get sick of her, but to say hatred? I don't think so, I don't think I ever grew to hate her, I loved her too much for that, I respected her too much, I admired her too much to stain all of that with cheap hatred, which our own unconscious develops as mechanisms of protection against ourselves. After hearing all of this, one might think that there's still some feeling in my words, but it's not like that at all. I've asked myself plenty of times, and honestly, I would never get back together with her. It's a closed chapter that I see as further and further away from my life every day, but I can't help but feel sorry about it . . . sorry for having failed, sorry for having allowed ourselves to lose so much respect for one another, sorry for not having ended it sooner, so that we would have hurt one another less, and especially sorry for my son. I think that if I ever get into another relationship, I would practice what I've learned: during an argument, the important thing is to listen and when somebody is very hurt or feeling a lot of shame, that is not the time to talk or try to fix things, because you don't make the best possible decisions at that time.

Albert's story is similar to that of many other couples who don't stop to think about why a relationship turns into a fury of arguments that provoke feelings that we've never felt or never imagined we'd feel.

The fact is that nobody wins any argument. If you think that you're right and you feel like a winner, think of how your partner feels. He or she may feel inferior or hurt, but it's unlikely that the argument changed his or her behavior or opinion.

Those Who Thrive on Arguments

Helen is twenty-four years old. She may seem young when she confesses that she likes to provoke arguments with her partner. But this relationship model is actually very common among couples of all ages. Many people erroneously believe that fighting fuels the passion in a relationship. Helen confesses:

Actually, I think I love fighting with my partner. I don't know why, but it's entertaining to me. But it's stupid because I like to argue alone, because actually my boyfriend figured this out about two years ago and he hardly ever argues back at me. But sometimes I make him explode with rage and that's when I ask him: Why do we always argue about the same silly things? Meanwhile I know that I'm the one who provokes it. Maybe I do it unconsciously because I'm looking to make up. But I think he's going to get tired of me one day. I think that, anyway, it's not good to argue all the time and I'm afraid because I've already set up this method of relating and I don't know how to have a healthier relationship.

This is one of many situations in which one or both partners seek conflict. In this case, the disagreement is blown out of proportion to the reality of the situation.

An argument is not a sporting event. You don't argue so that you can win, but rather to overcome a problem. If after the discussion you admit that the other person is right, don't see it as a defeat. Both of you came out as winners if, through the process, the conflict was resolved. When we feel as though we have lost, we feel vulnerable and later on we may become hostile and aggressive. This will lead to a bigger cycle of arguments. Ideally, an argument does not have to hurt anyone; on the contrary, it can simply be an excellent opportunity for discussing our differences and frustrations. This is the most reasonable occasion for communicating your disagreements. It is also an attractive moment for testing your progress in the area of personal growth, because it requires you to expand or restrict your point of view so you can consider your partner's point of view in the argument. In order to achieve this, it is necessary to feel appreciated and respected.

Situations That Contaminate Relationships and Lead to Arguments

Here's a list of the most common situations that cause or escalate arguments between partners, along with solutions for each.

Yelling: If the argument has reached a level of yelling, try to leave the space and find a spot where you can breathe deeply and count to ten. Once you're prepared to speak in a calm manner, do so and avoid offensive accusations, as these only worsen the situation. Both of you should make suggestions for improving your communication so that you can find a resolution. Yelling only leads to violence and accomplishes nothing.

Use a key word to help you get beyond the current problem. For example, when one of you has reached the point of yelling, use a phrase such as "positive energy" or "let's cancel this discussion." The idea is to eliminate yelling from the couple's method of communication. Yelling is a sign of insecurity. When you are confident about what you are saying, you express yourself calmly.

Refusing Affection: After a few years of living together, a couple may begin to notice that the hugs, kisses and sweet conversations are missing. Arguments often crop up from lack of affection. You cannot demand affection; you must try to recover those gestures that you once enjoyed together. A daily hug is comforting, a kiss makes us feel good and a kind word cheers us. It is extremely important to give and receive affection.

Avoiding Sex: Another problem that couples face is a lack of interest in sex, or periods of sexual incompatibility. Avoid using the excuse that you have a headache or feigning exhaustion to fall asleep early. The key is to talk openly about sex, be sincere and uncover what is causing the lack of sexual desire. It's wise to make some changes to intensify the sexual energy: try playing erotic games, exploring new times or places for sex, spending more time being intimate, using more erotic language and flirtatious gestures.

Lack of Appreciation: Do you appreciate yourself? It's a big mistake to think that your partner will appreciate you if you don't. Once you appreciate your own acts, others will mirror your example. You must take care of yourself by acknowledging your own worth, your special qualities and skills. In a relationship, there is a space that is shared between partners; but there is also a space that each partner can call his or her own, and that each must learn to value, nurture and respect.

Making Excuses: Although circumstances and our environment influence us, ultimately we are the only ones responsible for what we do. Excuses are seductive; they have a tremendous power of persuasion, especially upon our own ears. They offer precisely what we need, when we need it. They don't seem like pretenses but rather like sane and well-founded reasons. Before anything else, we must understand the nature of our excuses: how they function and how we create them without ever realizing what they are.

Who uses excuses? Not I, nor you. We don't use excuses, we use reasons. Therein resides the magic and force of excuses: our denial of them.

How do I get rid of my excuses? Think about why you haven't had any success; what is the reason? Let your mind provide all the justifications or necessary reasons for not doing it. Ask yourself "What's holding me back?" "Why is it so difficult?" "How important is it for me to reach this goal and what would be the benefit of reaching it?" Your answers may be the excuses that limit you; seek out these "reasons" and evaluate how many are real and how many are only evasions. Is it in my hands to work out this problem? What would I have to do?

FREEING YOURSELF FROM EXCUSES

Relax, close your eyes, think about your excuses and visualize them. Realize just how valid they really are. If you consider them to not be worth it, breathe deeply and every time you exhale move those images away from you, little by little, until they disappear or until you can barely make them out.

Now you're free of them. Relax and visualize the image of you having already achieved your goal. Breathe deeply and install this image in front of you. Feel motivated by it and satisfied that you can achieve it.

Unconscious excuses are a form of self-sabotage. When you discover an excuse, treat your mind as though it were a child, and simply show it the right way without making too much of a fuss. Act as if it were a game to improve your quality of life.

This will help you to avoid arguments and the need to defend what you've done and not done, because once you conquer your excuses, it's easier to do what's necessary.

Why Do Arguments Happen?

It takes two to get into an argument. Generally, the one doing the most talking is the one who is wrong.

When arguments cannot be avoided, it's usually because there are thoughts or emotional patterns in place that are harmful and toxic. These are triggered from within the inner world of one of the partners in a totally unconscious manner. It's as though this individual reacts like a programmed robot in the face of certain thoughts or emotions, and this provokes defensive and/or aggressive postures, as in the following examples:

The authoritarians: This way of reacting is caused by maintaining rigid and demanding rules about how things are supposed to happen. Any deviation from these norms is considered intolerable or unbearable, and brings about an extreme emotional altercation. This form of reasoning leads nowhere and drives the person to a series of judgments that alienate them from their loved ones.

Key thoughts: "You shouldn't . . ." "I have to . . ." "I don't have to . . ." "She or he has to . . ."

Advice: These people need to see things in a mirror. If they order you to do something, you should do the same to them, but without using an authoritative tone. For example, if she says, "I want us to visit this place," you reply, "Sure, if we can also visit that one." This will break down the authoritarian because she will feel that everything she asks for has a price that requires her to yield her authority. This mechanism will help the authoritarian to become more reasonable and humane. I don't recommend that you argue with this type of person, but rather break down his or her authority at every level. The model for arriving at a solution is: "I will do as you say if you do as I say."

Those who always have to be right: Being right can cause a similar sensation as winning a trophy, and some people lose all reasonable judgment. For example, a couple who is constantly arguing about the way they are raising their children, they can't agree on how to make love or how to manage money. It doesn't matter what the issue is, they always end up getting into endless arguments filled with lots of irritation. They can never reach an agreement. It's all just a power struggle, the goal of which is to emphasize that one is right and the other is wrong.

Key thoughts: "You are wrong," "I know what I'm saying; he's wrong."

Advice: In the case of this pattern, just humor the person, let him win the argument as though he were right, say "all right, sure," and then wait until both have calmed down before bringing up the subject once again.

Those who generate guilt: This pattern attributes total responsibility to others, without a realistic base. People project an imaginary or real misfortune without looking for a concrete cause in order to resolve a problem or conflict. For example, a man blames his wife for not teaching their children better manners; a couple blames one another for the problems that they're having in their relationship. Guilt frequently leads people to defend themselves, to act and think in an erroneous manner. Blaming others always creates a problem that is larger than the original conflict.

Key thoughts: "My fault . . ." "Your fault . . ." "It's because of . . ."

Advice: We must observe that if we're being blamed for a situation, a little inner voice also blames us and identifies with that person who wishes to make us responsible for all of his or her troubles. Automatically, negative emotions crop up and if we allow that guilty little inner voice to guide us, we will be consumed by it. Here's an exercise to help us modify this negative pattern:

TRANSFORMING GUILT

Sit down comfortably for a few minutes and think about the following questions so that you may learn from your answers:

- **Step One:** Focus your attention inside of yourself and complete the following phrase: *The guilt that I feel is like an inner voice accusing me of . . .*
- **Step Two:** Once you've listened to that guilty inner voice, turn it into an imaginary character. Keep listening to the little voice and pay attention to its accusations. For example:
  1. I am accusing you of . . .
  2. What I feel toward you because of this is . . .
  3. My manner of punishing you is . . .
  4. The rule you've broken is . . .
- **Step Three:** Beware of all of these phrases, as this will shed light on the code that is governing your subjective reality. Define as precisely as possible the code of behavior in question between the accuser and the accused.
- **Step Four:** Make a note of everything that the accuser says to the accused. Sometimes the accuser exercises some form of authority or domination over the accused.
- **Step Five:** Let the dialogue continue until the parties reach an agreement that both can consider acceptable. Both should be

clear as to whether the solution they've come up with is desirable, feasible or necessary.

By reaching an agreement, the conflict is resolved and the person feels liberated from the negative clutches of guilt. Once you understand this mechanism, you will no longer allow your partner or anyone else to manipulate you through guilt.

Those who don't trust: These people have a tendency to interpret the feelings and intentions of others without any basis. Sometimes these interpretations are based on a mechanism called projection, which consists of assigning your own feelings and motivations onto others. For example, a person is waiting for another person at a scheduled meeting time, and the person is five minutes late. Without reason, the other person begins to think: "I know that she's lying to me." This method of automatic mistrust is based on an inner lack of confidence.

The problem typically arises when people assume that others are going to take advantage of them. They fear that others will hurt them or deceive them. Many times they feel irrevocably wounded or offended by someone. They are quick to anger and react with hostility to what they perceive from others. These people are difficult to get along with, and their interpersonal relationships are problematic. This model of automatic reaction is based on an inner lack of trust. Their extreme paranoia and hostility may be expressed through demands, constant whining or hostile silence.

Key thoughts: "That's because . . ." "That is due to . . ." "I know that the reason for that is . . ." "He or she must have done this . . ."

Advice: If your partner mistrusts you, it's possible that you are not inspiring the necessary trust in him or her. Communication with this type of personality must be sincere and open. Here's a visualization exercise to help nurture inner trust:

EXERCISE TO NURTURE INNER TRUST

Step One: Breathe deeply and find a safe space inside yourself. It can be a cave, your home, a fortress or wherever you choose to imagine yourself. Visualize a place that inspires total trust.

Step Two: Once you feel yourself in that safe space, think about a situation in your past in which someone violated your trust.

Step Three: When you encounter that situation, imagine that a supreme sense of blessing invades you like a warm wave of compassion that descends from the sky. The sky represents your inner capacity for faith and love, the treasure that we all have inside.

Step Four: Feel how your heart opens and becomes filled with compassion, enabling you to understand all situations from the past in which your trust has been violated. Now release these situations; forgive yourself for any participation you may have had in it. As you recover your sense of inner trust, your ability to communicate will become more clear and sincere.

 The controllers: These partners wish to control one another through gestures and words. Maybe one person tends to always feel responsible for everything that happens around him. He may feel that his own well-being depends exclusively upon the actions of others, and he feels a need to control their lives. This individual typically feels that in order to satisfy his own needs, others have to first change their attitudes or behaviors.

Key thoughts: "If my partner changes her attitude, I would finally be okay." "I will only feel okay when so-and-so changes such-and-such." "I have to know what she wants so I can decide."

Advice: Create a well-defined area of personal space. When dealing with these people, it's essential that you set your limits clearly and remind them that they cannot run your life. Getting into a relationship should not be an annulment of your former self. If you let yourself be manipulated and controlled by your partner, you will end up feeling as if you have no freedom, and there is no way you can have a healthy relationship. Try to communicate clearly with your controlling partner that each one of you must take responsibility for your actions. Neither of you should be controlling the other.

The emotional manipulators: These people are characterized by their conscious or unconscious pressure upon others to achieve the things they want them to—even when it comes to the simplest details of daily living. Remember that with every manipulator, there is also someone being manipulated, and each partner suffers in different ways. The manipulator is functioning on the belief that obedience and submission are demonstrations of love. This is, of course, totally false.

For example, the manipulator overlooks the other person's feelings and concentrates only on acting in the way that he or she considers correct. Meanwhile, the person being manipulated will yield to the other's wishes in order to keep the peace. Such insignificant matters as what channel to watch on TV can generate conflicts.

What are the most common expressions of emotional manipulation and why does this manipulation have such an effect on us? Manipulators tend to abuse their partner's weaknesses and provoke feelings of guilt, shame or fear in the other person. They use everything they know about their partner to manipulate their emotions. They explode and lose control when they are contradicted; they play either victim or victimizer, depending on which is more convenient; they make their partner feel worthless when the person is especially weak or sensitive; they threaten their partner for no reason.

Key words: "If you leave, I'll kill you." "If you leave me, you'll never see your children again." "I always sacrifice myself for you, and you can never do anything for me." "If you can't accept this, I'll go look elsewhere." "If you leave right now, I swear that when you come back you won't find me here." "What would you do without me?"

Advice: The most essential tool for solving any problem is to accept the fact that the problem exists. Set limits to keep you from developing a relationship that is draining and dysfunctional. Express your feelings and communicate your needs without fear of what your partner may think. Remember that for every manipulator there is a victim. Stop yielding your personal power of self-determination to the other person. Never agree to something you don't want just to keep the peace. Extremes are dysfunctional: avoid attitudes that imply dominance and/or submission between partners. Recover the self-esteem that has been mauled by the manipulator and work with the inferiority complex that his or her behavior may have created. Turn to a professional therapist if you find it necessary.

 The false judges: This is the habit of seeing everything as unfair if it doesn't coincide with our own desires. For example, a woman calls off her date because she's tired and needs to sleep, and her boyfriend assumes that it's unfair of her to not want to see him. False judges also don't ask themselves who is right. They don't respect the other person, but demand respect for themselves.

Key thoughts: "They don't have a right to . . ." "It's not right that . . ."

Advice: Both partners in a relationship have to set limits. They have to express their needs and wants, and even their disappointment without feeling that they will be judged for it. If you are being judged in this way, you might ask yourself why you chose a partner who judges you instead of one who accepts you. Negative judgments have no place inside a relationship. Compatibility between partners is fundamental for a feeling of love and well-being. Mutual consideration is precisely what cements the trust between you, and it is this trust that will guide you toward the fulfillment of all of your hopes and dreams.

The chronic complainers: Complaints generally stem from our desire for the other person to embody our own ideals. Constant whining also results from not accepting reality. In a relationship, one person might be remorseful or complain that "I chose my partner because he was different from me, but now I want him to be like me because . . ." You can deduce what lies at the bottom of this conflict—the person selected somebody with the fantasy of changing him.

We might say that sometimes people break up for the very same reasons that they fell in love in the first place. We first choose our partners because they are our opposites, because they complement us and are therefore fascinating to us. Nonetheless, once the couple has spent some time together, frustrations begin to crop up. And for some reason, instead of seeking a way to work things out that would satisfy the relationship, the person thinks of changing the other, which is not only impossible but also conflictive. People with these characteristics cannot accept a more open-minded relationship.

Key thoughts: "I want it to be this way; I would like it to be this way." "I don't understand why my partner doesn't do what I tell her to do."

Advice: People remain in a state of chronic complaining because they don't want to change. They need to ask themselves, "How can I take responsibility for my own happiness?" It's important to analyze complaints in detail, as this is one of the most toxic mechanisms in relationships. What function does a complaint serve? Why do we complain? What do we want in exchange for that complaint? In reality, instead of activating our own resources for solving the problem, we complain to the cosmos, expecting something outside of us to come to our rescue.

The law of attraction is a spiritual and scientific key in life that is based on the following idea: One attracts what one transmits into the universe. It's like an echo: you will hear a repetition of what you project; it will be reproduced in your own voice. If you live in gratitude, you generate gratitude, and if you complain, you will attract more complaints into your life. In order to modify this mechanism and cast aside your complaints, it is important to carry out this ritual for freeing yourself from chronic complaining.

FREEING OURSELVES FROM COMPLAINTS

- Write down the things that you complain about in others. For example: "I don't like to get a rude answer when I ask a question."
- Next write down your own flaws, those that most people complain about in you; for example, the fact that you're always late for appointments.
- When your list is almost complete, try to see which elements are repeated in both lists. For example, "I don't like it when people are disorganized." People around me say, "I don't like it when I waste my time looking around for something I can't find." These factors resemble one another. You might say that they are the same mechanism because they demonstrate a lack of concentration or attention to daily chores.
- Now that you're a bit clearer on some of the problems, close your eyes and try to visualize yourself wearing a huge smile and feeling very happy. There are no complaints or negative ideas in your mind. You relate to others perfectly.
- Visualize inside yourself a white light that illuminates your partner and you. This light manages to make you feel satisfied and happy. Now illuminate your area of work. All the people that you work with are happy. Finish the visualization by illuminating your home and family. Observe everyone around you filled with joy and energy. This visualization allows you to unblock all the areas of your relationship, including work. You will feel yourself surrounded by harmony in any environment that you enter.
- If possible, place what you've written about your complaints into a bowl. Try to burn those pages in the fireplace as you end the ritual. Think as you're doing this that you have finally worked out the problem of all the complaining. You no longer need to complain; you now possess all your resources as well as the intelligence to solve any problem whatsoever.

The explosive volcanoes: These people wait passively for an issue in their relationship to change. They cannot express their discontent nor make suggestions. It's as though they are awaiting a miracle to fall from the sky and fix things. After a while, they suddenly explode one day without any concrete reason. Typically, they explode over trivial circumstances. For example, a man may wait for his wife to change a habit of hers that he doesn't like without ever making a comment in reference to it. One day he gets into an exaggerated, critical and heated argument simply because she moved her tooth-brush to a new location. This person seems unreasonable and irrational to her partner. Nothing is cleared up and the discussion makes no sense; one can't even figure out how it started. After blowing up, the person goes back to his usual passive attitude.

Key thoughts: "I can't understand how he or she doesn't see this him- or herself." "I can't understand how he or she can't know what I'm thinking." "It's obvious that if I looked at her that way, she should be able to guess that . . ."

Advice: Make it perfectly clear to these people that you have rights and don't allow them to shout at you or intimidate you in any way. Write down the following affirmations and post them somewhere in the house, where both of you can see them:

- My relationship is built on respect and is free of all signs of physical or emotional violence.
- I will not allow my partner to threaten me physically or verbally.
- I have a right to seek help for myself whether my partner wants me to or not.
- I have a right to study, work and lead a healthy life, with no interference.
- I have a right to protect the peace and harmony of my relationship.

It's a proven fact that when you write things down and express yourself clearly on paper, people respect your words more than if you had just said them verbally.

A relationship can be compared to the human body. In the physical organism, everything functions because every part of the whole has a role, and each is as important as the next. For example, skin cells serve the function of protecting, and even though they may be different from one another, none is more important than another. That is how love functions. Each person has to protect and help the other person so that the relationship organism can function. Each one must respect and understand what the other needs in order to grow as individuals and also as a couple.

Imagine what would happen in a body if all the cells began to argue over supremacy and power—death would occur in seconds. With our reactions being sparked without our wanting them to, without our thinking about it, without our being conscious of it, we contribute to the deterioration of the relationship; we drain it of passion, trust, friendship—and love begins to fade away.

FIVE GOLDEN RULES FOR ARGUING WITHOUT PROBLEMS

A couple's happiness depends on the way in which they argue and communicate. Sometimes this, rather than passion, is the central issue of a relationship. If you alleviate tension with laughter and ingenious phrases, the probability of success is very high.

1. Look into each other's eyes whenever it's time to express new ideas. An evasive glance, on the contrary, produces suspicion and doubt.
2. Maintain a favorable distance. If you're too far apart, you may have to shout to be heard and information can be lost along the way. If you're too close, the other person may feel crowded or that his or her space is being invaded.
3. Let the other person speak and don't cut off what he's saying. When the other person is finished, give yourself a few seconds

to make sure that he really doesn't have anything else to say before you begin. If you trample over his thoughts by talking over his words, he will feel that you're harassing him and that the discussion is going nowhere.

4. Don't finish the other person's sentences by saying what you think he plans to say or by "summing up" his thoughts. You could be mistaken and prevent your partner from communicating well.

5. Respect your partner's turn to speak. Monologues rarely serve to reach a satisfactory conclusion for both parties.

We never really know why we fall in love. On the other hand, we can conclude that we know why a relationship falls apart and breaks off. We defend ourselves against the enemy before us, we fear it, we hate it, we defy it, and we hurt it. The other person is our beloved, but the need to defend our own position and come out victorious becomes more important than anything else.

CHAPTER 11

I Love You but
I Don't Need to Possess You

Jealousy is a constant conflict in the heart of s/he who suffers it; it sickens the soul as well as the mind and our relationships with other people. Those who are jealous ask themselves: Is there any cure for this?

Jealousy: The Shadow of Love

Jealousy is the central theme in every soap opera and it is the most negative shadow in every relationship. Contrary to what one might think and to what is suggested by many song lyrics, novels and movie scripts, jealousy is not always the consequence of a very intense and great love, nor does it prove anything about how much one loves, needs or desires another. Those who suffer from attacks of jealousy are usually people who are very self-centered. Jealousy is based in a real fear of losing one's partner; it is our response to a perceived threat to our relationship. It becomes pathological when, on the contrary, the threat is actually imaginary. The problem worsens when the fury and intensity of the jealous rage goes beyond normal limits. Those attacks of rage and pain damage the relationship and turn it into a living hell. Jealousy can lead to domestic violence, and even crimes of passion.

Unhealthy jealousy arises when we stop seeing our partner as a subject and begin to see him or her as an object, as our property. This feeling of possession toward the other partner, the need to control, is accompanied by a lack of self-confidence, and feelings of envy toward the greatest riches in our partner's emotional life, such as friends and family members.

The Jealous Lover

People who are very jealous are often passionate, anxious and project their own tendencies toward infidelity onto others. They will go to great lengths to find proof of their presumed betrayal and resist rational arguments against it from those they trust. Delirious jealousy in which the person feels abandoned, unappreciated and betrayed may lead to the ultimate tragedy of perceiving one's beloved with hatred and feeling a need to attack him or her. This is why jealousy generates so many problems, not only in terms of physical safety, but in terms of the emotional equilibrium of others whose psychological state may be threatened by the situation.

Jealous lovers demand from their partners a detailed description of their supposed adventure. Fear mixes with ridicule in their minds—the fear of being talked about, the pain of feeling that the rival is worth more than they are, the loss of their self-esteem, an immeasurable urge to be in control, an exacerbated sense of possession and aggressiveness toward oneself. They live out the situation as though it were torture and they often have the desire for vengeance, which can include anything from the need to enclose oneself in silence to the drama that is so often described in news headlines.

Some people admit their jealousy (often in a scandalously loud voice) while others brood in silence. If you think your partner might suffer from unhealthy jealousy, here are some signs to watch out for:

- The person needs to have total control over everything her partner does.

- The person considers her partner naïve and gullible.
- She doesn't like it when her partner goes out alone or with friends.
- She doesn't like to see her partner wearing provocative clothing.
- She makes scenes in public places without reason.
- She believes she knows her partner's secret intentions.

There are many different types of jealous lovers. See if any of the profiles listed below are familiar to you, and refer to the solutions for how best to negotiate with these people.

The Obsessive Possessive: This person's jealousy is not limited to members of the opposite sex. This person cannot stand the thought of *anybody*—be it a friend, family member or pet—taking up his partner's time and attention.

The solution in this case is to stand up to the person by setting your personal limits and refusing to go along with any demand that seems unfair to you or curtails your personal freedom. The possessive lover will often make unreasonable rules, such as "you can't go out with your friends" or "you must be home by a certain time." And it's likely that if you refuse to follow these rules, the person will make your life miserable with an endless string of accusations that you must not take to heart. He may also punish you by refusing to speak to you, perhaps for hours or days. The best thing to do in the face of this type of behavior is to ignore it. Like a child, the person will eventually get over it.

The Compulsive Spy: This person will snoop through your organizer, your address book, your calendar, your e-mail and wherever else he believes he can find out what you're doing behind his back. The worst part of living with this is that when the partner complains of being spied on, the compulsive spy will answer, "Aha! Now I *know* you're hiding something." It's a no-win situation. This type of behavior pattern is particularly difficult to manage, but you should set some sort of trap for him to keep him from accessing your personal things. For example, change the password that opens your e-mail account. Once the person is subtly reprimanded in this way for invading your privacy, either of two things will happen: if he is not totally compulsive, he may feel shame at what he has been doing and stop spying; if, on the other hand, the person has a real problem, you'd do best to see a couples therapist and try to work through the dynamics that exacerbate this behavior.

The Lover Who Threatens to Leave: This jealous lover warns you that the worst thing you can do is lie to her. She insists that she would never forgive you if you cheated, and that she would immediately leave if she found out. The person continues to affirm this without any reasonable necessity, constantly threatening to abandon the partner that in fact has never cheated. Like most other types of jealous lovers, this one also feels a need to control her partner's life. The best way to handle a situation like this is to ignore the threats. In fact, of all the people I've known who suffered from this pattern of behavior, none ever actually left.

The Suspicious Mind: This person constantly fears and believes that his partner is secretly pining away for some past lover. He is threatened by everything that his partner may have shared with other lovers and would like to wipe out every memory of past love. The worst part of this scenario is that the person is driven to ask questions that he really cannot stand to hear the answers to. At the same time, he can't stand the thought of not knowing every intimate detail of his partner's past romantic encounters.

You have to be brutally honest with this kind of person. Do not allow him, under any circumstances, to make up ideas or stories about what you've done in the past, or what you are secretly wishing to do again. The idea is to prevent yourself from constantly having to defend yourself and your right to your own memories.

The Raging Explosive: The behavior pattern that this person presents is sudden attacks of jealousy that motivate a huge scene in any given location. The person makes outrageous accusations and imagines things that have no basis in reality. This person will turn any incident into a potential motive for a fit of jealous rage. "Oh? Suddenly you're into action films? Since when?" or "So you have a new coworker? Is she single? Is she attractive? Is she after you?" These questions and comments are typical in this scenario, and it seems as though the jealous partner only wants to complicate the circumstances more and more.

For some people, it is more desirable to have a violently explosive confrontation every so often than to enjoy the tranquillity of a calm and stable relationship. The adrenaline produced during a fit of rage can feel like pumping excitement. In cases like this, I suggest you seek out therapy, because the cycle of raging explosions can eventually become more dangerous and even life-threatening. You may need to choose a different partner if you really want a life of harmonious love instead of suffering.

Catalina, age thirty-five, complains that her life became a living hell when she and her partner reached the point of irrational jealousy:

When I started my relationship with Albert, everything seemed normal. In fact, our relationship was the envy of all my friends. He was very attentive and romantic; he would give me flowers almost every day and he always had time for me. I was very happy with him. Everything started one day when he showed up at my house and I was there with an old friend of many years whom I hadn't seen in a long time. He walked into my house and made a terrible face and was very rude to my friend, so that my friend left right away. Once we were alone together, I asked him what was the matter and he told me he couldn't stand the idea of seeing me with another man, to which I answered that it was not "another man" but an old friend of mine from school. He became furious and started to tell me that I could not have any close male friends because men always wanted something more.

From that moment on, everything changed. I could no longer get together with my friends, even if he was around. This played itself out in a very strange way. If I wasn't allowed to have any friends, then he also would not be allowed to have any friends. We spent two years in seclusion, concentrating only on each other, as if the rest of the world had disappeared.

Our relationship became a terrible spiral. One day on campus I saw him talking to a classmate about some project they needed to do. In my insanity, I forbade him from doing the project. Finally, our relationship just died and I was left absolutely dried up. None of the restrictions that we imposed on one another worked out—his jealousy triggered my jealousy and both of us ended up out of whack.

Jealousy is a natural part of any relationship. The euphoria of feeling like the single most extraordinary being in our partner's world dissipates upon the appearance of a third party. In a couple it is important to respect one another's freedom, emotional states and basic needs. As soon as one of the parties feels as though he or she is the owner of the other's feelings, the balance of the relationship is disrupted and jealousy appears.

Edward, age forty-one, admits that he is possessive by nature, and describes some of the feelings he experiences when attempting to control the jealous impulse:

I am jealous and possessive. Sometimes I get really rude and I know it, but the problem is that when I fall in love with someone I feel like that person belongs to me, like part of my own body. I feel jealous just think-ing that they might smile at someone else. I imagine things; I guess I weave stories in my head . . . It's strange to feel like you own somebody, when in reality they're not yours. I have doubts about whether or not she loves me. I feel distrustful when she smiles at other people, when she makes ambiguous comments to her friends, even when I can't make sense of them. I'm observing the changes in her all the time, which lead me to believe that there's another man. Where is the love? Where are all those caresses and eternal kisses? Where is that thing that I can't find in her?

It wasn't always like this . . . or maybe I just didn't realize . . . Today

*I am, and . . . I know what you're thinking, Mabel, as I'm telling you
this: that everything is inside of me, that the love for myself is what I
put onto others, and I can even say I'm conscious of it, but I'm jealous,
compulsive, excessive, passionate and crazy. That's just how I am, and
that's how I manifest myself. So, from this point on, I will try to control my jealousy, to not be affected if someone else is looking at her. I
will be careful, I'll be aware of her movements but I won't let on that it
matters to me that there's a world around her. It's bad, I know, but
what can I do?*

I worked with Edward on a series of visualizations to help him
better understand the things from his past that provoke such instability in his relationships. The exercise I suggest in this chapter,
along with the one I describe later in the book on the inner child,
both helped him to become more conscious of his subjective reality
and enabled him to make his current relationship more open and,
ultimately, more stable.

As we've seen, jealousy breaks up and torments relationships.
Jealous individuals end up draining the pleasure from their relationships with their obsessive drive for possession and smothering per-
secution. To survive, a couple requires tenderness, understanding,
tolerance and respect for one another's autonomy.

Here are some tips to remember whenever you feel an attack of
jealousy coming on that threatens your emotional well-being:

- It is essential to be conscious of jealousy, without attempting to
  fool yourself.
- Communicate your feelings to the person whose behavior has
  generated the feelings of jealousy, specifying very clearly the
  conduct that made you feel jealous.
- Discriminate between what is false, real or imagined regarding
  your partner's behavior.
- If it's an irrational thought that you're nurturing, it is important
  to see the reality and uproot the idea once and for all.
- Rely on your partner to help you process your feelings. But don't

forget that he too is being affected, and you should try to understand and help him.

- Invite your partner to discuss personal subjects and speak openly about issues in his or her past that were perhaps too painful to talk about or have been silenced by fear or shame.
- Share intimate thoughts and experiences under the condition that there will be no criticism or negative comments made by either of you. If you put up unconscious barriers, cast them aside consciously.
- Try to understand more deeply how the trust that each partner has in the other functions. How far does our loyalty or lack of trust go?
- It's never too late to rectify negative attitudes. If you demonstrate your willingness to change your negative habits, your partner will have no difficulty in following suit.
- Trust allows for total freedom for each partner to have his own set of friends and to develop his own interests, without it meaning that he cannot share many moments, friends and interests with his partner also.
- Come up with a balanced distribution of your time. Both you and your partner should have periods of separation to do things individually, aside from the daily chores of living together.
- True love can only exist and last between two people who feel successful as human beings, who have absolute confidence in themselves and who extend that level of self-confidence to include respect for their partner.
- In cases where you cannot manage your jealousy, seek the help of a professional in the field of psychology.

What Do We Do with Jealousy If It Persists and Doesn't Allow Us to Love?

People who are jealous have some sort of inner mechanism that prevents them from giving of themselves wholly; instead of surrender-

ing totally to love, they hold back and give only fragments of themselves.

- This person loves his or her partner, but doesn't trust in the reciprocity of these feelings.
- This person demands understanding from his or her partner,
  but is incapable of comprehending that the partner is also a
  human being with his or her own set of needs.
- This person assumes that his or her partner possesses amazing
  attributes, yet fears that these very attributes will cause the partner to leave the relationship.
- Even if the person's capable of recognizing the reciprocity in the
  relationship, he or she unreasonably fears losing his or her
  partner.

What causes this fragmentation of the self when giving? Why is
there this need for some sort of guarantee? People who are extremely
jealous are perceived by others as immature and domineering. A
relationship filled with jealousy cannot possibly function like a
healthy adult relationship between two people who complement
and complete one another physically, emotionally and spiritually.

These attitudes often end up destroying the relationship. The
jealous lover believes that nobody can ever be trusted, and as a
result, every relationship is doomed to fall apart. Every attempt at
love yields the same results, causing a terrible cycle of insecurity that
always leads to disappointment.

Is there a way out of this cycle of jealousy? It appears that the
only open door is through the realization that the problem lies not
in your partner, but in your own inner fear. Of course it's never easy
to see this. That fear is unconscious and those who suffer from irrational jealousy really believe that something outside of themselves or
some omnipresent force is causing their relationships to fail. The
only way to break the cycle is to journey through your inner self to
determine how much of your behavior is caused by your partner's
actions and how much is caused by your own insecurity and fear.

The Roots of Jealousy

Here is an exercise that I successfully use frequently with my clients. Find a space where you can relax for about twenty minutes. Before beginning, do a few of the relaxation exercises outlined in this book. Perhaps work with your breathing as described in the segment on anger (following this segment) before carrying out this visualization. After the relaxation exercise, follow these instructions:

Step One: Once you're totally relaxed, concentrate on the situations that provoke jealousy in you. Then notice the thoughts that come to your mind. Those might be:

- My partner doesn't love me anymore.
- My partner's looking at other people because he or she no longer desires me.
- My partner's leaving me.
- I'm no longer important in his or her life.
- Why does he or she talk to other people?
- My partner no longer trusts me.
- It's been a long time since my partner told me he loves me.
- He goes out with his friends more often than with me.
- She doesn't have fun with me like she used to.

Step Two: Reflect consciously. The aforementioned examples are thoughts and doubts that may come up in your mind. The first thing you must remember is how much of those thoughts may be a projection of your own fear and desire. If after meditating on the thought, you still believe it's something concrete and real, you should do another relaxation exercise and think: "In this relationship in which I feel jealousy, at what point did I surrender my power and self-worth, like a child who depends strictly on his or her parents?" Continue with your meditative state.

Step Three (protecting your vulnerable self in need of love): While you're relaxed and focused, visualize the most vulnerable part of yourself, that part that is fearful and jealous—it can be a stage or period of your life, yourself in the present or some image from the past. Observe the state of your emotions. Don't worry if you feel or see images of insecurity, fear or abandonment. Imagine yourself taking that vulnerable version of yourself into your arms and protecting it, giving it all of the love that it needs.

You have to be very aware of your true needs, every demand, so that you may learn to understand how to help yourself. Surely that which your inner self is demanding of you during meditation is the same thing that you usually demand from other people.

Use a notebook to write down the date and record your responses to emotional situations after doing the exercises. This way, you will be able to track your emotional progress. You will be surprised at how, after practicing these exercises, your loved ones will begin to change their attitudes and to manifest more positive feelings toward you. You'll also see how your self-esteem will improve and your emotions and thoughts provoked by jealousy will dissipate day by day once you free yourself from making so many demands. The important thing is to repeat this same exercise every time you feel jealous.

CHAPTER 12

I Love You Enough to Overcome My Anger

Every human being has the right to feel rage, but that doesn't give you the right to be cruel.

Anger and Its Consequences in Relationships

Anger is one of the most common emotions among human beings. Some people seem to live constantly in this state, but all of us get angry on occasion. It is perfectly normal to feel anger or rage—our response to this emotion is what matters. The big problem here might be that every time we get angry, we allow ourselves to automatically be swept away by this emotion and cannot get past our feelings. Frequently anger is accompanied by thoughts of vengeance and this can lead us to humiliate, criticize, judge, offend, bother and even hate another person. We may feel guilty about it the whole time, or become increasingly incapable of living peacefully in the world.

The consequences of our anger, depending on the degree to which we are able to manage it, can become extremely important. For example, if my boss, secretary or coworker does something to upset me that I am not able to manage, I could easily transfer that to my partner or my children. This needlessly causes a deterioration of our intimate relationships.

The question is, what can I do about my anger? Learn to manage it. As stated earlier, it is not wrong to feel anger; what's important is our response to it.

In order to manage my anger, the first things I must ask myself are:

- What good is this anger doing me?
- What thought patterns have led me to this state of rage?
- What consequences might arise if I don't manage my anger?
- How can I transcend this emotion right now and think clearly?

If you're convinced that the anger does you no good, it's time to analyze the origin of this emotion: when, why and how it comes up. What are some of the associations that trigger it? What are some visible patterns in your behavior and how can you understand them by relating them to similar situations in your past?

Learn to Breathe and Free Your Anger

The power over our emotions lies inside each one of us. When you feel anger that you cannot seem to manage, do the following:

- Breathe deeply once or twice with your eyes closed.
- Explore your body and find where the anger is hiding; generally it's in the chest, solar plexus or abdomen.
- Now that you have located the anger, color it black, as if it were a dark cloud of smoke.
- Start breathing deeply, noting how the breath leaves your body every time you exhale.
- Continue until the emotion has calmed itself and left your body.
- Now feel the sensation of peace and tranquillity in your body and realize that you can control your emotions.
- Open your eyes and observe the world around you through more loving eyes, accepting the fact that nobody can create your anger.

This exercise is very easy since it can be done in a few minutes, when getting into the shower or anyplace where you can be alone. Go back and talk to your partner after you do it. Once both of you are feeling calm, tell your partner what he or she said or did that made you angry. You will probably be surprised by your partner's response. Perhaps you misinterpreted his or her motives; perhaps he or she too is feeling sorry about having been so impetuous and would appreciate the opportunity to apologize.

Repressed fear often leads to irrational anger. Susan is twenty-five years old and suffers from fear of abandonment. She wasn't aware that her emotional needs were being expressed through her anger, and that this was seriously damaging her relationship. Even when we can observe our process of getting angry, it's not always easy to see the root cause of the anger. Susan's story serves as an example:

I realized that I tend to get mad just as my partner is leaving for work or to be with his friends. I'll find an excuse to make him stay and then I'll go into my long face, monosyllabic answers, crossed arms, cutting remarks—I mean, the works! Then, as my anger escalates, he'll say that he's leaving, that he doesn't want to make me mad, and that I need to calm down and he'd better go. I go on pouting, telling him that I'm really sorry, but all I need is a hug. The sofa is where we make up. By this time, it's all tenderness and patience, with gentle kisses on my back and him caressing my legs. He'll remind me that if that's all I want, I should just tell him or take the initiative instead of wasting half an hour making him try to figure out what he's said or done to make me mad.

This game of anger and manipulation is not the best for provoking romantic or sexual desire in one's partner, nor is it effective at getting the other person's attention. It might work to some benefit maybe two or three times, but in the long run, the other person will figure it out and become tired of his or her partner's infantile demands.

Susan worked with her inner child using the exercises that I explain in Chapter 14 to sort through her hidden emotions and arrive at the cause of her anger. This helped her to understand and control her fits of rage.

Forty-year-old Alex realized that he had been transforming the stress and tension from his job into anger in his personal relationship:

I am ashamed to admit that my constant anger and my frustrations at work were my biggest problem in my last relationship. I never communicated with my partner, neither about what I was thinking nor about what I felt, nor why I would always get unreasonably angry in any frustrating situation. Is it insecurity? Is it fear? Perhaps, but I don't like to feel vulnerable in front of my partner. I don't like her to know exactly how I feel, and I think this situation makes me lose out on great relationships. The idea that men aren't supposed to be fragile has always affected me a lot.

Alex's experience is also very common in relationships. People with an emotional block that prevents them from knowing how to express their feelings and/or ideas end up frustrated. Many people convert that frustration into anger.

Verbalizing Anger

One thing people do with their anger is cover it up. Think of the pressure that builds up inside a pressure cooker when you tighten the lid; it's extremely powerful, right? Fortunately, there is a method for "decompressing" these emotions. It requires that you face your anger and release it through communication.

Let's say you come home from work in a bad mood and any little thing that your partner says or does makes you feel irritable. Instead of allowing your frustrations to escalate into an eruption, let the emotion come out in a controlled manner. Express what you are feeling verbally to your partner. Try saying, "I'm in a bad mood right now, but it's really not your fault" or, "Let's talk about that after I relax a bit." After controlling the anger for fifteen or twenty minutes, the negative emotion is likely to have dissipated a bit.

Be sure to verbally express your discomfort in a direct manner, but without aggression. Explain your feelings to the other person directly and without fear. The other person may see things your way if you are able to explain what's going on with you. Express your feelings at the moment—don't wait until later. To hold a resentful grudge will only serve to have your feelings come gushing out all at once in the next argument. Avoid negative comments and aggression. The person receiving this aggression will be put on the defensive and the two of you will end up in a battle. On the other hand, the person may shut down, which will also not get you what you want. Try to confront your partner in a tranquil and calm way; defend your point of view always, but show respect for the other person, who also has a right to an opinion.

Another acceptable manner to release anger is to talk to yourself out loud. The sound of your own voice combined with the relief of talking about your feelings will keep further tension from building up inside you. End your talking session by repeating affirmations such as "I feel relieved now."

Accept the fact that nobody can make you feel angry, happy or sad. Nobody can fabricate an emotion inside of another person. You alone have the power to create an emotion inside of yourself; therefore you are the only one who can eliminate it.

Calming Volatile Emotions

Emotions have long been considered a mystery, especially when someone notices in himself an emotional imbalance or the presence of irrational emotions. Below are some tips to help you control your anger and to nurture your feelings of love and peace:

• Try to stay calm when some external stimulus provokes fear or anger in you.

- Control your language and use discipline when expressing your emotions.
- Project positive mental images onto the situation.
- Evaluate the emotions that you may be provoking in others.

Try to breathe calmly and slowly whenever you confront an emotionally challenging situation.

Healing Wounded Relationships

In order to lead your relationship from a path of hostile aggression to one of harmony and full acceptance, you need to heal the emotional wounds inside of yourself. Eliminate anything that prevents you from respecting and accepting yourself.

You may use the following steps to reestablish respect and appreciation in your partner.

1. **Discover and heal the wound.** Understand that you are having a conflict in your relationship because it has reactivated some underlying pain inside you. To heal the wound, you must first face the fact that you allowed yourself to be hurt; this will help prevent your resistance to affection and harmony and lead to a truce in your relationship.

2. **Control your thoughts.** For example, a wife may feel that her husband is selfish and doesn't care about her needs. She could go down a list of things in her mind that her husband has done to demonstrate his concern and consideration for her. This would allow her to formulate a different thought pattern along the lines of: "Okay, so he does usually care about me, but this particular thing that he did was inconsiderate." This way of thinking opens up the possibility of reaching a positive outcome through dialogue, whereas the other fuels resentment and anger.

3. **Accept full responsibility for your part in the lack of respect and affection.** Relationships are a fifty-fifty collaboration. Each

person has to put in 100 percent of his or her energy and effort to make it work. Once you realize this, you will understand that you must confront your own patterns of behavior before you can expect change from your partner.

4. **Forgive yourself.** It is not only important to forgive the other person, but to forgive yourself as well. By opening your heart, you can understand the situation that hurt you or caused you to feel negative feelings such as anger, shame or pain. Once you understand the causes of your distress, you can understand the other person better as well. When you forgive yourself, the conflictive emotions inside you that germinate anger and resentment begin to dissolve.

By following these steps, you learn to nurture the more loving aspects of the relationship and heal the damage that hostility and aggressions have created.

CHAPTER 13

I Love You and
Our Communication Is Perfect

The best skill to have in a relationship is to know how to manage conflicts. Every couple needs to know that disagreements are part of a relationship, and thanks to this we grow and exchange ideas and feelings, and end up winning in love.

Assertive Communication

Words are not swept away by the wind. Words leave scars; they have the power to influence us positively or negatively. Words may either heal or hurt a person. For this reason, the ancient Greeks believed that words were divine and philosophers revered silence. Think about this and be careful with your thoughts. Your thoughts turn into words and words set up your destiny. Meditate wisely about when and how you communicate. Silence might be the best gift you can give yourself or your loved ones. Communication is the tool we use to transmit information to another person, yet in interpersonal and sexual relationships, very few people know how to communicate effectively and intimately with others.

Assertive communication is the ability to develop an effective exchange with another person. Assertiveness is a way to establish relationships by speaking from our own feelings directly, respecting our position as well as that of others. Assertive communication is both verbal and nonverbal, honest and measured on behalf of all those involved.

We have to understand that a conflict in a relationship is normal. You cannot stop speaking; you must learn to recognize that the relationship will continue in spite of the problem, the anger and the conflict, so communication cannot be suspended. Life's other issues must be handled as though there were no existing conflict. It's important to take into account the following points that contribute to good communication.

When arguing with your partner, use phrases such as "I think, I believe, it seems to me . . ." and don't generalize. Focus on the problem and not on accusing or harassing the other person. For example: "I would like to have the meeting take place without interruptions," rather than "You're always interrupting the meeting." Evoke facts and not judgment. For example: "You were twenty minutes late, and this happens every time that we have something important to do. I want you to know that this issue affects me every time it repeats itself because I don't like showing up late to appointments or keeping friends waiting for us." Instead of: "You have no consideration for anyone! You don't care how much it bothers me when you're late." Be clear about your requirements. For example: "Please make an effort to leave work a little earlier. That way we can enjoy one another and be more relaxed at dinner." One of the most common problems in communication is generated when someone attempts to read somebody's mind or expects somebody to read hers. If you want people to respond to your ideas and needs, you must say things just as they are, and express yourself in a way that allows others to respond favorably to you.

The Power of Words

The power of words is one of our greatest human gifts. Words are capable of perfectly expressing our thoughts; they reveal our inner world and are the most powerful tool for maintaining lasting relationships.

The language we use guides our relationships in specific directions and helps us shape our reality, optimizing or limiting our possibilities. The ability to use language with precision is essential to a couple's communication.

Here are seven rules for improving verbal communication in your relationship:

1. Be careful when using the words *no* or *don't*, because they can lead to the opposite of their intended effect. For example, think of "no": nothing comes to mind. Now, try this: Don't think of the color red. I asked you not to think of the color red, but you probably did. Try to form your sentences using positive and not negative phrases. Instead of saying, "Don't talk to me that way," try, "I'd like it if you'd say that to me differently."

2. Note your use of the word *but*, which negates everything that came before it. For example, "He's a wonderful guy, but . . ." Instead, substitute "and" for "but" whenever you can, and you'll notice a positive difference in the way that others interpret your comments.

3. Talk about your problems or negative characteristics in the past tense. When you transform your verbs from the present to the past tense, you are programming your mind to send your old limitations to the background and focus on new ideas in the present as a means of bringing about a positive change in yourself. For example, you might say, "I used to have trouble with . . ."

4. Refer to the changes that you hope to bring about in the present tense. For example, instead of "I'm going to achieve . . ." say, "I am achieving . . ."

5. Use "when" instead of "if" when referring to your plans and goals. For example, say, "When we save the money, we'll go on a trip," as opposed to, "If we save the money . . ."

6. Replace "I hope" with "I know." For example, say, "I know I'll

learn," instead of "I hope I'll learn." The word *hope* implies doubt and weakens the assertiveness of your language.

7. Replace the use of the conditional tense with the present tense. For example, replace the phrase "I would be thrilled to see you" with "I'll be thrilled to see you."

By learning to speak clearly, positively and correctly, we can tap into our inner power of manifestation by altering our subjective reality. Words have tremendous spiritual power in a relationship. Try doing the following exercise with your partner:

Sit facing one another and take turns asking the questions that each of you needs to ask in order to evaluate how your erotic and emotional relationship is doing. After each partner responds, the other should thank him or her for the answer. This is a great way to open up to each other. The questions might be along the lines of:

- What do you expect from our relationship that we haven't achieved yet?
- Do you think that everything we are doing in the relationship is helping our bond to grow stronger?
- We share a wonderful bond, but should each of us be giving more of ourselves to the relationship?

Try to answer succinctly, for example:

- The aspects of myself that I've given to this relationship thus far are . . .
- I would like us to have greater intimacy in the form of . . .
- I want to feel more fulfilled in my life in the following ways . . .

Continue asking the same question until there is no more left to say on the subject. Once you finish, try to find the points that you see similarly and those that proved surprising or challenging. By doing this exercise frequently, you can dramatically improve communication in your relationship.

Heartfelt inspiration expressed through the spoken word produces pleasure and wards off emotional pain. The power of words dominates the soul and transforms our inner reality like a magic spell.

Nonverbal Communication

Nonverbal communication is one aspect of human relationships that is rarely taken into consideration. This includes glances, touch, movement, gestures, facial expressions and posture. Body language occasionally underscores verbal insinuations, and at other times may lead to intimacy and emotional communication.

Remember that whenever there are inconsistencies between verbal and nonverbal language, the nonverbal cues actually have more impact on the transmission of the message than do the spoken words. Avoid situations in which these inconsistencies create problems. Nonverbal gestures are processed in a special area of the mind. Those that are appropriate to the words being spoken serve to accentuate the verbal message received, so make sure that your gestures and body language emphasize what you really want to communicate. Don't transmit contradictory messages with your gestures. If you are looking around the room or fidgeting when you say something important, the person listening to your words will have a hard time accepting the sincerity of your words.

To use assertive nonverbal communication, heed the following examples:

- Keep your body firm while attempting to clarify your point of view, but maintain a relaxed posture and serene attitude.
- Don't stand too close to the other person. You could make her feel as if you're invading her personal space.
- Look into your partner's eyes (not too deeply, because the other person might interpret that look as aggressive). While talking, you shouldn't be looking around at other things like the window or the ceiling.

- Don't cross your arms. As long as you keep your body open, it will be easier for you to understand the other person.
- If you cover your mouth while speaking, you may give the impression that you are lying or that you are withholding something important.
- Be conscious of your head's movements. If you move your head in an affirmative way, you may reveal different messages according to the rhythm. Nodding rapidly means: "I understand, go on." Or it could mean that you want the person to hurry up and finish what he's saying. When your head moves moderately, it is saying "I understand and agree," and when it moves slowly, it means "I understand but I'm feeling a little confused" or "I'm not totally convinced of this." Inclining the head is another gesture that can be interpreted in different ways. An inclination toward the front or side means "I'm listening." When accompanied by a smile and eye contact, it's augmented by feelings of sympathy toward the other person and increases the probability of receiving support and cooperation. When your head is inclined toward the side and back, it means "I'm thinking over your question," and a clear inclination to the side means "I'm interested and maybe even attracted."

Every detail of your gestures provides others with information: "I care about you, I'm keeping you in mind, I want to give to you, I want the best for you, I accept you, I acknowledge you, you exist," and so on.

Communication without Guilt

Try not to blame your partner or attack him or her as if you were fighting a war. Remember that the other person is your partner; therefore he or she is automatically on your side. For example, also express the positive feelings that you have toward your partner while addressing any negative attitudes. Always speak in the first person. Don't just say "You make me uncomfortable, you make me unhappy." Say instead, "I feel confused, I feel unhappy." This will make your partner more likely to listen to you without feeling guilty or responsible for your feelings.

Learn to appreciate the other person, because while your partner has needs, anxieties and negative moments, you have them too, and perhaps you don't realize how patient the other person is being with you.

The Other Side of the Coin

Your partner should know that he or she can tell you anything because you will pay total attention. Knowing how to listen will allow you both to communicate better, to create special bonds of complicity between you and to know what each one wants, needs or is worried about. Practice using this magical phrase: "I'm listening . . . tell me about yourself." How many times have you used the following phrase with a friend—and how about with your partner? "Tell me what's going on with you."

Put Yourself in the Other Person's Place

Your partner cannot nor should behave exactly as you do. To get angry over everything your partner does without trying to understand or change is a mistake. Even though you should have certain similarities, there's no need for you to think alike. Understanding this will help you to be much more tolerant with one another.

It's also very important to remember to say "Thank you!" We all need to be appreciated. There is no better way to tell someone that he is important to you than by saying "Thank you." Don't just thank the person mechanically; do it warmly and authentically.

Understanding Freedom

This is one of the most difficult aspects of any relationship, since normally even if we want it for ourselves, it's very difficult to grant our partner freedom. Each party has the right to his moments of independence and intimacy, to pursue his own projects, interests and illusions without feeling limited by the other person. Although the contrary might appear to be the case, controlling your partner, wanting to constantly be with him or to keep him from doing other things because of your own insecurity, will drive him away from you. The most generous and beneficial position for the relationship is to support your partner in a constructive way as far as his or her individual development.

Be Willing to Reach an Agreement

Communicate the problem by asking for the necessary help to resolve the conflict fairly. It's fundamental that both parties understand that a problem that affects the relationship cannot be resolved by only one of the parties. When trying to tackle the problem, use skills to help benefit the solution as much as possible. Maintain an active posture, suggesting possible solutions without discarding anything beforehand. Don't let problems persist without a resolution. Specify what is bothering you; try to isolate it from the other components that may lead you astray. Choose the correct moment; avoid bringing up a problem when the other person is tired, sick, when there are other people around or when you just don't have enough time available to finish the discussion.

We must never forget to say, "Help me, I need you." When we cannot or don't want to admit or express our frailty or need for others, we are in grave danger. Don't repress yourself. Ask for help!

Affection Before, During and After

Maintaining affection during any conflict is very important. A lack of affection brings about the end of many relationships. Affection is the demonstration of love, and is fundamental once the infatuation and passion begin to diminish in the relationship. Not feeling loved is one of the all-time most common complaints among women.

Affection is something that has to be nurtured daily, since it's the easiest thing to lose over the course of time. You know your partner so well that you don't believe it's necessary to offer affection and flattery. If you're not receiving affection, you have to let your partner know in order to see if it's simply a matter of taking things for granted or if there is actually a deeper cause.

Affection doesn't just have to be physical—it can also be verbal. The most important thing about saying "I love you" is that no human being can feel really happy until it is spoken to them. Dare to tell your partner, your parents, your siblings or your children, even if you've never done so. Try it and check out the results. Each party in the relationship has some quality or characteristic that deserves special recognition. Try saying: "I admire you," "You're special," "You're unique." Everyone, at some point in his or her life, feels the need to be recognized for some achievement or success. When was the last time you did this?

Reconciling with Yourself and with Others

It's not always enough to be forgiven by someone else; sometimes you have to learn to forgive yourself. Negative emotions are the result of psychological programming from the past, related to our childhood. If we don't clearly understand our negative emotions, they become toxic. This exercise will allow you to heal negative emotions that don't let you reconcile with love. This is a process of evoking emotions. It's a subtle way to start to understand what is happening to you and why you repeat certain relationship patterns. Sometimes we are angry and argue with our partner, and then realize that what is really required is for us to make peace with ourselves.

TRANSFORMING NEGATIVE EMOTIONS

Step One
- Get into a relaxed state.
- Close your eyes.
- Now look through your memories and choose a person who evokes an emotion in your life that provoked frustration, aggression or anger in you. (This can be your current partner, or someone else.)

Step Two
- Look into the eyes of the person you are remembering.
- Recognize the emotion(s) in his or her eyes. (If the other person doesn't allow you to look into his or her eyes, then go ahead and feel the emotions created by resistance and separation.)
- Feel the equivalent emotion inside of yourself.
- Try to feel that the emotion felt by the other person is the same as yours. Don't allow for any resistance.
- Recognize the emotion and release it as though it were a wave passing by or a cloud floating overhead.

Step Three
- Are there any other emotions coming up now? Work through this emotion in the same manner.
- Give the other person a hug.
- Open your heart to the other person, and allow your love to flow toward the open heart of that person.

- Make sure the person returns the love, until the love flows freely between the two of you.
- While the love is growing, try to observe yourself inside a circle of light, as though inside the sun.
- Feel the solar light cleansing all of your relationships and any negative emotions that you might feel toward anyone.

Step Four
- Now imagine that your shared negative experiences over time have created cords of energy between you.
- Visualize these cords as black strings formed by the arguments and misunderstandings between you.
- Take a step back from the other person.
- Feel how the sun's light cleanses the energy between the two of you, freeing all the cords that united you.
- Now make sure that the energy is totally cleansed.

Step Five
- Create a new cord of glowing light between you; it can be the same solar ray as before.
- Imagine that from the heart of the other person, and from your heart, a giant pink ray of light is emitted, liberating all resistance between the two of you. Allow the pink light to cleanse any resistance in your heart.

Step Six
- Thank the other person for the lessons you've learned from them.
- Liberate the other person with love. Feel the physical sensation as you release the energy from the other person.
- Once you feel ready, slowly return to your normal state of consciousness.

This internal process of cleansing toxic emotions will attract more and more experiences of love, pleasure and harmony into your life.

In order to nurture positive and assertive communication, we must think in terms of "we" and not "I" and anchor ourselves in the awareness that we are partners working toward the same goal.

CHAPTER 14

I Love You and
I Want You to Humor Me

Humor is the closest feeling to love, because it allows for many different levels of communication. It always starts with a smile. Afterward, the soul sees the beauty of that which made it smile. In this game of humor, you manage to inject joy into areas that you would have never thought.

Using Humor to Awaken Our Inner Child

A sense of humor and a smile are natural and innate in all individuals. As years pass, people often lose their sense of humor and laugh less; they lose the ability to play, to see the humor in things. Facts and circumstances taken too personally affect us and provoke stress. That's why it is so important to keep your inner child alive, and maintain its innocence and capacity to laugh and love. In the next section of this chapter, we will explain what the inner child is and what kind of emotional functions it carries out in our lives.

A Sense of Humor

Humor is important to your relationship. It allows you to battle conflicts with the unfailing weapon of cheerfulness. Naturally, a good sense of humor is usually one of the first things we look for when seeking a partner, whether on a personal or a professional level.

Being jovial protects the relationship because the ability to laugh and to demonstrate affection is the greatest formula for repairing a relationship after an argument or crisis. One cute comment, a funny joke or a simple smile may become a decisive element in winning someone over no matter how difficult the situation or lover's quarrel.

A sense of humor is like a sixth sense. Many believe that this sense protects us like a talisman from stress, heart attacks and misfortune, both present and future. The more evolved people are on a spiritual and emotional level, the better their sense of humor. They don't personally identify with circumstances and know that they can shape their own destiny by maintaining a lighthearted attitude. Therefore, they don't become uncentered by negative experiences—nothing can separate them from their unique and special essence as an individual.

Yet, as with all things, there is a limit to how far humor should go. Constant joking can become a barrier to speaking seriously about certain subjects.

What Is Your Sense of Humor Profile?

Sense of humor is difficult to define. This is because humor has a lot of different meanings. Among the most common profiles are:

Responsive: People who easily detect and enjoy the sense of humor in others or in a funny situation and respond to it without reservations.

Senseless: People whose laughter points out the absurd in circumstances or people.

Ironic: They have a subtle genius and generally play easily with words. They share their humor with others.

Sarcastic: For many, this is the negative version of ironic humor; these people laugh at the negative in others and at their expense. Many times they assume a position of power to make fun of others.

Hostile: Tending toward mockery, making fun of people, and generally aggressive jokes and pranks. These people are good at laughing at others, but usually not willing to laugh at themselves.

Those who laugh at themselves: For many, the most mature form of humor is reflected in their ability to laugh at themselves without fear of feeling ridiculed by others.

Paranoid humor: People who suffer as a result of other people's sense of humor, because they feel as if they're being made fun of. People like this will walk by a group of people and if they hear laughter coming from the group, will feel terrified and ashamed. This is usually linked to some negative experience from childhood.

Humor:
Another Approach to Pleasure

Joy is an unconditional feeling that fine-tunes the deepest fibers of your heart, generating beautiful, melodious, incomparable desire for the one you love.

People react to sexual jokes either with nervous laughter or in a fun way, but this is only the instinctive reflex that each person uses as a means of release, because through laughter, a person can channel and release hidden tensions arising from the sexual energy that is repressed inside.

The use of humor in a sexual relationship is a different and very healthy tool for lovers. Jokes with an erotic charge can break up the monotony of daily conversation. By encouraging lighthearted communication about sexual attitudes, these humorous exchanges can free up stored resentments.

A good sense of humor enables lovers to be playful as they exchange pleasure with one another. Have you ever tried enjoying sex while mixing in humor with eroticism? Have you ever considered sharing erotic jokes plus sex, caresses, whispers and moans of pleasure with your partner? When sexual communication gets blocked up, have you ever tried saying something funny?

By adding laughter, couples feel safer in their sexual and emotional relationships. Humor mixed with sex is a combination so perfect, in fact, that it manages to relax and release the entire body, warding off pain, frustration, fear and stress, and producing an overall sense of well-being. In our bodies, laughter releases a double dose of hormones and sexual vitality. Cultivating a great sense of humor is important to every aspect of your life.

Below are some of the benefits of having a good sense of humor:

- It attracts and retains love.
- It empowers your health and sexuality.
- It strengthens individual and shared motivation.
- It stimulates innovation.
- It optimizes internal communication.
- It helps to integrate relationships.
- It strengthens relationships.
- It creates a more pleasant and humane environment.
- It generates innocence and expands our learning capacity.
- It allows our ever-present inner child to play.

The Fascinating Inner Child

When blocks occur in our relationships, it's fundamental to get in contact with our inner child, that vulnerable, sensitive part inside of us that didn't get enough love as a child and needs attention. The inner child is that part of us that can help us resolve problems that originated in our childhood and affect us as adults. The work involved in getting in touch with our inner child has to do with reprocessing different stages of our emotional development, especially those experiences that were difficult because the stimulus we received was too intense for us to manage at the time. We can say that the inner child lives in our hearts and needs certain things to stay alive. The most important thing that this child needs is love. He or she also needs to feel comforted in the face of conflicts and during painful situations and to be reassured that emotional wounds from the past will not recur. This child needs to express his or her feelings about painful memories to someone who will listen and understand. Perhaps that child remembers having to accept love in a manner that did not genuinely fulfill his or her needs; perhaps the child modified certain aspects of his or her behavior out of fear of being violated, suffocated or ignored.

The inner child is the pure and infantile part inside each of us. This part is not only fragile; it is also magical and has a magnificent capacity to probe deeply, to compress information in a simple and accessible manner. In many cases, for any number of reasons that might have occurred during childhood, that child has not been able to manifest and is waiting to be loved, recognized and accepted.

Think of your inner child as someone who lives in your heart, wanting and needing certain things that allow you and him or her to go on living. This part of us needs to express its feelings and wants to be understood. This child feels more comfortable around other people who are open and can tune in to his or her feelings. In a healthy relationship between partners, there is plenty of caring and sharing, but usually on an adult level. If you want your relationship to be stable and offer happiness to both of you, then you must begin to know and heal your inner child. Furthermore, if you have children at some point, this internal process will help you to better understand them.

Gabriel is a young man of thirty who is warm, intelligent and a bit shy. He recognizes that when he was a child he felt rejection from his father. As an adult, he unconsciously attracted a partner who has many of his father's characteristics.

I remember how my father would get angry and become totally furious for no reason. As I was growing up, I was always afraid that I would repeat that behavior, but instead I attracted my wife, who gets angry very easily, sometimes seemingly for no reason. Now I'm working on the fear of repeating the cycle of anger with my inner child. When I feel like my wife or anybody is about to dump their rage or some negative energy on me, I take my inner child into my arms and remind him: "This is not about me, and it has nothing to do with you. This person is merely expressing their pain and it's all right." That technique seems to have helped a bit to ease the pain that I felt when my wife got angry at my kids over something that was pretty insignificant. It kept me from feeling resentment and I think that by my not reacting to it, she was also able to contain her anger a little bit.

At some point, we realize that we attract those people whose issues remind us of some episode that we were never able to resolve during our childhood. There is a lesson to be learned through this.

Characteristics of the Inner Child

Friendly and cheerful: Children by nature believe the world is a friendly place. They have hope and everything is possible. This innate optimism is an essential part of our nature, yet it's also an element of what is considered childish.

Innocent: Children live in the moment and they're oriented toward pleasure. They do not distinguish clearly between good and bad. At first, their movements seem to lack direction, because they're so interested in everything that it's hard for them to focus on one thing. That's why children venture into forbidden places, touch objects that are uncertain and taste new things.

Dependent: Children cannot fulfill their own needs by way of their own resources. For this reason, they have to depend on others to take care of them.

Emotional: Emotions are not blocked in children. They can experience emotional extremes, laughing, crying or feeling pain, all while continuing to play.

Open and flexible: Children are open and flexible because they have the ability to constantly adapt to new situations. This is because they are not attached to the past.

Untiringly playful: A child's ability to play and have fun is limitless when compared to an adult's because the childish imagination is fundamental. If we consider infancy to be an essential period of free creative play, we can see that all of us have the capacity to play.

True to oneself: Integrity also makes children special, extraordinary and unique. As adults we may sometimes lose our innate freedom to express ourselves fully and to take refuge in our own hearts.

Spiritual and magical: Spirituality involves a sense of connection with something larger than we are. Children are naturally full of faith; they know that something exists that is greater than them.

Imaginative: Children have the magical ability to use their imagination to resolve problems.

Capable of love: Children love in a natural manner, without knowing or judging. Love simply expresses itself through them like a free-flowing channel. Emotional blocks against feeling and loving emerge later, once the child has been exposed to social and cultural conditioning.

WAYS TO MAKE YOUR INNER CHILD HAPPY

Here is a list of some activities that the inner child needs in order to feel satisfied:

- Being at home with the family and feeling the warmth of home
- Being in contact with nature and experiencing a spiritual and physical connection with Mother Earth
- Being appreciated and loved by friends and loved ones
- Not making rash decisions
- Keeping the physical body in excellent condition
- Feeling trust and compassion for others
- Having one's physical senses stimulated by beauty—for example, a beautiful view, fragrance, or flavor
- Developing new talents and skills
- Being oneself
- Going to an amusement park

Pleasing Your Inner Child

It is always important to please and delight your inner child, to spoil and care for him or her. Those little things you do will make your relationships easier and make you happier. Below are some examples.

- Treat yourself to a favorite toy: a doll, an electric train, construction toys, a dollhouse, a yo-yo, a kite, a hula-hoop, soap bubbles . . .
- Throw a costume party.
- Do something artistically creative and enjoy playing with the materials. For example, spend one day a month playing with paint, clay, ink, or finger paints.
- Discover things that make you feel happy. This could involve dancing, bike riding, having guests over for dinner, going to the

movies to see an animated film or making a video with your kids.
• Read a few of your favorite books from childhood.

When I started working with my inner child, I found a book of fairy tales that I used to read when I was little. While reading the magical roles of each character, I remembered the tremendous capacity that we had as children to fill every space, every moment, with an adventure out of our own imagination. In this way, we were able to take any situation and transform it into a fabulous adventure.

From my perspective, our lives improve on every level once we start to work with our inner child, not only on a personal level, but also in dealing with our partner. Imagine what it would be like if your partner could once in a while become like the best friend you had as a child—someone with whom you play and make up parallel realities. It would be so special and enriching as adults to take the time to dream together. Have one play the role of the adult and ask the other what he or she wants and vice-versa, or have both of you connect with your inner child at the same time and just play.

Connecting with Your Inner Child

Never forget to take your inner child by the hand wherever you go. Never let him or her disappear from your life. My inner child is always with me. I guard her and protect her, and she provides me with the happiness and faith that I need. It is essential to take time to devote ourselves to our inner child. No matter how old you may be, inside of you there is a little child who needs love, acceptance, play, distraction and laughter.

Step One: Find an adequate location in which you can be totally calm. Relax or do one of the relaxation exercises.

Step Two: Try to remember some moment in your childhood when you had a problem or when you felt that your point of view was very important. For example, you moved to a different city and had to attend a new school. Maybe a new sibling was born and you lost some of the attention from your parents. Maybe your parents told you something that caused a conflict between you and them. Maybe there were nutritional problems, or something else. It can be any episode that happened between infancy and age twelve.

Step Three: Once you remember the incident, try to relive the event and see how that child felt inside. Visualize the child, but also think and feel what the child thinks and feels. Identify with him or her; look at the world through his or her eyes. Feel in your body how that child experienced those childish emotions. Respect and allow every sensation that arises in your body and try to be conscious of your thoughts.

Step Four: Ask the child different things depending on the incident, but always address him or her in a loving tone. Try to understand that child; is he sad? Maybe he needs something. How can you best satisfy or care for him? Simultaneously play out the role of both the child and the adult; no one knows this child better than you. Allow the child to play and express himself but don't stop asking questions: what would he like to do? Or what does he need to say? Why didn't he have the nerve to do or say this at the time of the incident? Note how that reaction that the child had or the decision that he made has influenced your relationships in your present adult life in either a positive or a negative way.

Step Five: If the promise or decision that the child made to him or herself at the time was negative, explain that she didn't have options back then, or didn't know enough about life to have made a better decision. But now she has the opportunity to change and to stop suffering. Calm and comfort the child. Apologize. Tell the child how sorry you are for having abandoned him or her. Assure him or her that you have been negligent long enough and are now ready to make up for it.

Step Six: Promise the child that you will never again abandon it. Tell the child that he can reach out to you anytime he needs to, that you will always be there for him. If he is frightened, hold him in your arms. If he is angry, tell him that it's all right to express anger toward you and that he doesn't have to be afraid to talk to you about it. Don't forget to tell him how much you love him.

Step Seven: Once you've advanced to this point and understand perfectly that the child is doing what she needs to do and is calm and happy, talk about your desires as an adult. Share your dreams and aspirations for right now, in the present. Discuss your plans and ideas regarding your work, your relationship or anything else that means a lot to you. Your inner child can help you, through his or her magic, to manifest those dreams that you desire. A lot of blockage occurs when your inner child disagrees with the decisions you are making as an adult.

Do your best to meditate daily, talk to your inner child and check in constantly with his or her emotional state. If you do this every day, even for just a few minutes (while traveling or before you leave your house, or maybe just before you retire at night), this will become one of the most powerful things you can do to build confidence and self-esteem in yourself, especially if you want to be open to loving yourself and others.

When you feel blocked in your relationships, go straight to your inner child and ask him or her why you feel that your emotions are blocked. What does he or she need to express that you as an adult are not allowing? Allow the child to express his or her answer through physical sensations such as pain in the body or by reliving scenes of past memories. Your inner child will always respond with the truth and will surprise you as children are apt to do, because he or she always sees life as something new. In contrast, as an adult, you don't always see things as clearly as the inner child, because you assume you know everything.

Healing the Inner Child

Kim, age thirty-nine, describes how she overcame conflicts in her life by working with her inner child:

My mother married my father when she was very young. When I was born, they left me at my grandparents' house. My grandparents were somewhat well off. I lived with my grandparents until they died when I was thirteen years old. I lived in a home filled with love. Once they died, I went to live with my parents and my younger brothers. My father was abusing my mother mentally and physically. When I was eighteen, my parents split up. My life was pretty difficult at that time. I got married at age twenty-one and had my first child. I got a divorce when my son was fourteen years old. That same year I graduated from college and started working. It was hard for me to work because I didn't have anyone to help me with my family, since my mother has never been much help. After a while, I met a man who offered me moral support and fell in love with me. I was a very fearful and insecure woman, always feeling lonely, empty and sad, until I began to work with my inner child.

The Dialogue with My Inner Child

My inner child appeared to me and I asked her in my adult role: "Do you miss your grandparents?"

"Of course I do," answered my inner child.

"Why don't you call them?" asked the adult.

"They're not around anymore," answered the child. "They're in Heaven."

Then the child went on. "But there are things that I will never forget: my grandmother's green eyes, my grandpa's gentle voice . . ."

"Call them," I insisted in my adult role. "They're still alive in your heart."

Suddenly my two grandparents appeared on the scene, hugged me tightly and expressed love for both the child and adult parts of me. I felt incredibly happy, as though the old wounds in my heart had suddenly healed.

I meditated on those hugs for a pretty long time, almost three months. I saw changes taking place inside me, and in each conversation I had with my inner child, I was able to perceive that she was vibrating with happiness. I felt calmer and happier every day, and the new relationship I had just embarked on suddenly began to work out perfectly.

Now I realize that my inner child is a very real part of me. The best things in my life continue to flourish inside of me because the seeds of love that my grandparents planted have continued growing and I feel loved. I especially feel loved by me.

It's fascinating when you manage to discover the importance of your inner child in your life and your current relationships.

CHAPTER 15

I Love You and
I Want to Shower You
with Tenderness

Tenderness is not just a physical thing. It is a delicate sensation, a spontaneous emotion, a feeling that overtakes and heals the heart of its old invisible wounds.

Tenderness:
The Recipe for Lasting Love

How do you define tenderness? We could say that tenderness is a sensitivity that springs from the soul and expresses itself through the body. This feeling is special and is a natural gift that creates an inner state of harmony and compassion between two people who love each other. You can also feel tenderness for everything that exists in the universe.

True tenderness is given and received in a spontaneous fashion, but people who exhibit this characteristic also know how to recognize, accept and remain open to affection given to them. Tenderness is not like passion, which explodes like a volcano and then burns out like a match. Tenderness envelops us like a warm lake that purifies and remains calm while encompassing the skin and heart.

Tenderness between lovers is evident in the largest and smallest of details; it is delicate, soft, warm, translucent and suggestive. It may be a shy glance, a carefully timed caress, a surprise kiss.

Sometimes, due to the constraints of time, tenderness is neglected. The woman expects tenderness from the man, and the man dreams of it without saying anything. In both cases, tenderness creates an atmosphere of companionship, of knowing that one can count on the other beyond sex and passion. It's important to express tenderness naturally and at all times, but above all, during moments of crisis. True tenderness breeds harmony between partners.

Review the past few days in your mind and ask yourself how many times you wished that the person that you love would surprise you by taking you into his or her arms. How many other times have you longed for tenderness in your relationship? Social conditioning, especially among men, is the largest cause of this problem. It has made us believe that tenderness is a form of weakness. Tenderness is not a weakness; in fact it demonstrates strength of heart. Tenderness is an adaptation to life's cycles, while coldness and lack of affection represent a block produced by fear of feeling love, or of being rejected when we express our feelings.

Many of the problems among couples originate from not knowing how to make love, not in the sexual sense, but in the emotional sense. Love is built from acts that demonstrate love: tenderness, kisses, gifts, details, hugs, caresses, looks, dancing, seduction. To achieve tenderness requires an awareness of all these important elements and a commitment to behaving this way on a permanent basis. As I have said in many of my books, nobody has taught us how to love. Nobody ever explained to us how to make love last, transform itself, expand, change, grow and not exhaust itself. What are the factors that nurture relationships so that they shine, become free and produce pleasure in our lives instead of pain? Of course, crisis is a natural part of a relationship. All of us go through different complex circumstances, but if we resolve these issues with respect, consideration and tenderness, everything will be far easier to overcome.

No relationship can last without caresses and tenderness, without the desire to kiss, the need for companionship and the pleasure of closeness. A caress acknowledges the lover's body with desire, as a source of pleasure, as an indispensable space in which love ceases to be a mere word and becomes part of human reality.

When you dare to express your affection for your partner in a spontaneous way using looks, gestures and smiles—from the firm and delicate caress to the vigorous embrace, warm kisses sprinkled with simple and frank words—everything becomes easier and the journey becomes filled with happiness.

The Tender Embrace

Physical contact and stimulation are absolutely necessary in order to make us feel loved. An embrace as a means of communication expresses that which cannot be said with mere words. A hug provides feelings of pleasure; it can be superficial or deep, but it is laden with pleasant emotions. To place your hands around your lover's neck or waist and bring your faces together constitutes a demonstration of love that is as necessary to us as the air we breathe.

Jackie is thirty-two years old and has been married for eight years. She learned that tenderness is a key ingredient in maintaining a passionate and loving relationship:

When my husband hugs me, it makes me feel protected. His tenderness surfaces when I lean my head against his shoulder, and this gentle breeze just wraps me in a fantasy as though it were the first time we ever touched. After eight years of marriage, every time he hugs me and kisses me in that special way, like he used to in the beginning, I feel my body floating with delight. Eventually he looks at his watch because he has to go to work or something, or I have to go pick up the kids from school, and everything ends pretty quickly, but boy would I love to spend more time in his arms, kissing and hugging like we used to do when we had nothing else on our minds.

Many couples don't believe that they have the time for tenderness and sensuality. They should therefore set aside some time to preserve this very special sensation of loving and feeling loved.

There are many things that both men and women need in spite of our much-touted differences. None of us are totally exempt from the yearning for happiness that can be found only in a harmonious partnership. And this is due to our need for tenderness. Every one of us needs that quota of protection and affection, whether it's a loving hug before going to bed or a friendly embrace that offers you support after a hard day at work. Only our beloved partner knows how to make us feel totally secure.

There are many ways to hug and to transmit sensations through an embrace. A hug provides energy and encouragement, a feeling of comfort during positive as well as negative moments. It comforts us in our sadness, celebrates our euphoria, expresses congratulations and affection or appreciation. Hugs can vary according to their intensity. The stronger the hug, the more energy it transmits. It can range from a pat on the back to a passionate embrace, the kind that leaves a mark deep inside . . . the kind that gives you a shot of positive energy.

Visualization:
The Tenderness in You

Do one of the visualization and relaxation exercises. Sit or stretch out in a place where you know nobody will bother you. Slowly close your eyes and relax. Allow your mind to be flooded with thoughts of tenderness—those moments in which you have hugged or kissed someone you desired. Remember also concrete situations in which you have not been able to express your love. Now imagine that you can express it, and that that person will feel the vibration of love that you are sending him or her in the present. Time is not important when it comes to love, because love is timeless. The important thing is that you have realized your own need, and that person will vibrate with you in harmony and peace. Now visualize a crystalline light that penetrates your heart like a pure harmonious wave. Feel the tenderness of the entire universe empowering you. Repeat this exercise every time you feel the need for this tenderness.

Gestures That Express Tenderness

A caress given at just the right moment encompasses the greatest of our human emotions. Thus it is important to know how to caress and be caressed, to flatter and kiss our loved one. How many times have we bypassed those marvelous moments of tenderness that include the following acts:

Holding hands: Lovers love to feel one another's skin in their hands as they walk down the street, or anytime they want to feel as though they are one being. Interlacing their fingers expresses the passion and tenderness that each one feels toward the other.

Caressing the cheeks or face: This gesture expresses stability in the relationship and the sensation that your partner is passionately attracted to you.

Sincere flattery: It can be a cute come-on such as "You look hot in that dress," or "Your eyes are lovelier than ever," "You're as beautiful as the first time I saw you." Flattery provokes self-esteem in your partner and is something you should practice every day of your love life.

Pat on the thigh: This is a way of saying "I desire you," and both men and women will receive the gesture with pleasure and joy. It is also a spontaneous gesture among couples that says, "You are sexy and you are mine."

Playing with your lover's hair: Both sexes play with their lover's hair to express tenderness and interest in their partner.

The lover's glance: You can actually caress your lover with your eyes and become lost in the other person. This way of expressing love is the best kind of body language that we can offer as a gift of affirmation. Both partners enjoy it when their loved one looks them in the eye when it's time to express something. This seemingly small detail is capable of melting anybody with love.

Kissing: There are as many types of kisses as there are needs to express feelings of passion, tenderness and sensuality. A kiss given with true tenderness is a loving and refreshing gesture that is perfect any time of day.

Hugging: Hugs provide a plethora of benefits. They erase the feeling of loneliness. They help to assuage fears. They open the door to loving sensations and stimuli. They boost self-esteem. They slow down aging, help to reduce anxiety and are so gratifying that, in fact, I'm running off to hug my husband right this minute.

Sending e-mails or leaving little notes: Send a kiss or say "I love you." A quick e-mail or short note that expresses your feelings goes a long way toward letting your partner know how much he or she means to you. You don't need complicated words; just state your feelings. How are you feeling about him or her at that moment? "I can't stop thinking about you"; "I miss you"; "I need you." Or send a cute emoticon by e-mail. Don't wait for a special occasion to say "I love you"; surprise your partner any day of the year.

It's incredible how the energy of tenderness works like magic. As I was writing this segment, my husband called me while traveling on a business trip. I was very concentrated on my writing when I answered. He said, "Hi darling, how are you?" I mumbled a few words in response and then said, "All right, you're distracting me, but you haven't cut off my inspiration for writing this book, so I will stop and talk."

"I can call you later," he replied.

"Darling, I'm writing about tenderness. If I don't behave tenderly toward you, the person I love most in the world, I shouldn't be writing this book. I love you."

He laughed and took great delight in my comment.

Part Two

SEXUALITY: NOW WHAT?

I lament the opportunities for making love that I let go by because of pressing tasks or puritanical virtue. . . . Sexuality is a component of good health; it inspires creation and is part of the pathway of the soul. . . . Unfortunately, it took me some thirty years to discover this.

—Isabel Allende, from her book *Aphrodite*

deal and many of the prejudices surrounding sex have been abandoned. In today's society, sexuality maintains a massive presence and has infiltrated its way into everything, especially the mass media. Sex has been unleashed and exposed for what it actually is: a source of powerful energy that facilitates a person's ability to feel happy and more complete.

Physical and Spiritual Satisfaction

At some point in our history, sex began to be seen merely as a means for obtaining physical pleasure and for procreation. All of the spiritual implications of lovemaking were cast aside.

Yet practices from ancient Eastern philosophies integrate the physical and spiritual planes of reality. The immediate goal of these ancient practices is to learn the art of giving and receiving pleasure. On the physical or sexual plane, this could mean discovering how to give yourself pleasure, how you like to be caressed and where your most erogenous zones are. Exploring the mysteries of your own erotic nature will allow you to later communicate your preferences to your lover so that he or she can explore your pleasure along with you. Both sexes benefit from this practice. It increases and develops tactile sensitivity as well as orgasmic potential. It also eliminates old stigmas, shameful secrets and taboos attached to our own pleasure. Masturbation is sometimes used as part of the personal development process in these ancient practices, and these techniques are called "sensual self-stimulation" or "waking the inner lover."

This concept of the inner lover is not related to narcissism, but rather to a spiritual quest. The more you love yourself the more confidence you have in yourself, and the better your possibilities for success in relationships and in everything that you do. Like your inner child, your inner lover is a part of your own nature. This is the part that guides and counsels you, gives you pleasure and is always there for you. This is that little voice inside you that helps you overcome

I Love You and
I Burn with Desire for You

Sexuality gives rise to the miracle of life. Through sexuality creation is made possible, and that is why, though we may attempt to deny it, sexuality governs a very large portion of our lives.

Sex after "I Love You"

As the love in our relationship is established passion flourishes, and along with it, the desire for deeper and more satisfying sex with our partner. Sex is one of the most important subjects in a human being's life; it is also one of the most conflictive. In spite of what most people believe, sexuality is not separate from spirituality, nor is it something to be ashamed of. It is neither reserved exclusively for procreation, nor is it a mere instrument of pleasure.

Throughout history there has been a lot of interest in censoring the divine art of sex. From the beginning of human existence, it's been known that the sexual impulse had to be repressed in order to maintain order. Yet in spite of everything, human beings have not resigned themselves to keeping quiet about it. People continued to openly and privately discuss the mysteries of the human body and the pleasures provoked between men and women.

Without a doubt, the opinions of this world have changed a great

moments of sadness and stress; it gives you strength and allows you to live life to the fullest.

The object of waking the inner lover is greater spiritual abundance, greater self-love and a greater consideration of your body as a sacred temple of love. This contact also increases your possibilities of finding a real lover, as it allows you to see everything that you are capable of giving to yourself as well as to those around you with greater clarity. The idea is similar to an inner marriage—finding your perfect inner lover and then learning how your actual partner manifests those characteristics. This helps you to be more conscious of what you expect from your partner and vice-versa.

CONNECTING WITH YOUR INNER LOVER

All of the wizards, saints and prophets who have investigated the path of true spirituality have concluded that the kingdom of the divine resides within the self. It is through your inner lover that you will begin to understand your capacity for giving pleasure, affection and delight to yourself as well as to those around you.

As I explained in the previous segment, sex is not merely a physical need—it is externally physical and internally spiritual. These two aspects are not separate entities at all; they are only perceived as separate by the mind. The discovery of our inner world offers us security and allows us to identify and receive exactly what we need sexually on both the physical and the spiritual plane. Below we will describe the steps necessary to explore the inner lover in each of us:

Step One: Find a comfortable spot where you will not be interrupted for fifteen to thirty minutes. Initially, it is important to practice this exercise while your body is resting, at least until you manage to achieve a style of breathing that is natural and fluid. Breathe deeply by inhaling and exhaling with your lungs and your entire abdomen. Your breathing should begin in the pit of your belly, using your entire capacity to take in air, and exhaling very slowly and calmly, relaxing all the muscles in your body as you exhale.

Step Two: Pay attention to your thoughts and allow them to sweep over you like a shower of energy—don't attach yourself to any one thought. After a few minutes of relaxation, place one hand over your abdomen and the other over your chest, exhaling all of the air slowly and gently through your nose, emptying your lungs completely. Try to keep your lungs empty for a few seconds. Inhale gently, inflating only your abdomen, until you feel the lower portion of your lungs fill up with air. Without any effort, you will feel your diaphragm expanding downward; during these moments, the lower and middle regions of your lungs are filled with air.

Step Three: It's important that you take advantage of the moment just before exhaling to empty out all your thoughts and imagine them being liberated along with your emotions and daily tensions. Then, bring the air up to the upper region of your lungs, contract your abdomen slightly and let the air out little by little. Repeat this process for a minimum of ten minutes.

Step Four: Now visualize yourself in an empty space (the air, or a cloud, for example) and relax your entire body there. You can also imagine that you are on a beach or some other place that you love.

Step Five: Now try to move within that space; being conscious of each movement, begin moving different areas of your body. Start with the simplest, such as your arms, legs and hands. Then move on to more specific complex areas such as your fingers, toes and eyelids.

Step Six: Now imagine your inner lover in that place within your mind. It doesn't matter what gender appears in your virtual space, just concentrate on making your lover feel happy. Try to see your lover clearly, connect with him or her and ask the questions you wish. Find out what your lover needs, and how he or she feels, and what he or she likes. What does your inner lover need for you to do in your visualization to make him or her feel truly loved, on both the emotional and the physical plane? Listen quietly to your inner lover's responses, and experience the sensations they cause you to feel in your body. It is essential for you to understand what your inner lover truly needs so that everything you do will manifest as pleasure and love in your external reality.

Practice this exercise two or three times a week to better understand your sexual needs. This is especially true if you do not have a partner, as this process may help you find your ideal partner by enabling you to seek out someone who is totally compatible with your personality, whose ideas are similar to those that you have discovered regarding what makes a relationship passionate and harmonious. Keep a dated notebook and record your experiences. This way you can analyze and observe the development and evolution of your inner work. This exercise can be done either as a couple or alone.

If you are in a stable relationship with someone, it is important for both of you to do this work together. One of the members of the relationship may act as a guide, leading the other to the ideal mental state in order to encounter his or her inner lover. The guide should lead the other person along without any attachment to ideas or judgments, so that the inner world can manifest in all its fullness. The guide should also not make comparisons between the descriptions of the partner's inner world (images that come up during the visualization work)—whether emotional or physical—and the images that the guide sees and feels.

The person who is being led should answer the guide's questions and connect to the inner lover while in a relaxed state, with eyes closed. You should never do this exercise without later switching the roles, as each partner should be equal. If you suggest doing the exercise together and your partner refuses to do it, you should just continue and start doing it on your own. But remember that doing it as a couple will help both of you reach full communication and improve your overall relationship.

Florence is forty-two years old and like many women in traditional cultures, she has not accepted her sexuality as natural. She felt inferior to men and her self-esteem as a woman had been decimated, until she discovered her inner lover and found true love by learning to love herself:

I always had a lot of problems accepting my sexuality. I was basically comparing myself to men but didn't realize it. I was totally compulsive and addicted to sex and love. I could never stay with anyone for more than two or three years, and I was already almost forty. The fear of growing old and not having found emotional stability worried me.

While doing the exercise for connecting with the inner lover, I discovered that the figure inside of me was a woman who was absolutely vulnerable, stripped of self-confidence and love. I took care of her, asked her what she needed and what she wanted. After working with my inner lover for about seven months, three times a week, I got to know her and learned to accept her and to offer her the love that she was needing. I was able to feel far more stable and didn't really need to go to bed with the first man who came along. I could spend long periods of time alone without feeling anxiety or fear, without distracting myself by going to parties or attending unnecessary events which were really not leading me anywhere.

After a few months, I was at a gathering of friends and I met a man who seemed very vulnerable, almost feminine in his features, and seemed to be very sensitive. Any other time, I would have rejected him unconsciously, because he seemed far too similar to that part of my own personality that feels denied. But after doing the work with the inner lover, I felt attracted to him. Now we are a very happy couple and everything's going well in my life: sex, affection and a deep friendship between us. My partner understands my most vulnerable areas, and that's why I no longer have to pretend to be strong like I always had to do before. I lost the need to be in control in my relationships and I gained the love I now feel for myself. My sexuality has changed; now I can relax and feel my partner much more deeply, because even though I have had many sexual experiences, I think that never before had I allowed anyone to actually penetrate my heart.

By awakening our own inner power, manifesting our love with physical and mental satisfaction, we approach happiness, sowing the seeds for a satisfying relationship with both ourselves and our partner.

CHAPTER 17

✦

I Love You and I Love Pleasing Us Both

While making love to myself, my body vibrated in front of the mirror.

While looking into my own eyes, I found the image of your eyes filled with passion and fire. I exploded in a sea of pleasure.

Even though you were not present, your hands led mine down the path of total pleasure and together we enjoyed the magic of love.

Pleasure Trip: Alone or with Someone?

Every romantic relationship between human beings starts with the self. The first form of sexual contact is autoeroticism—self-stimulation or masturbation—and is one of the most elemental, though no less satisfying, sexual practices that a human being can enjoy. It basically consists of stimulating one's own genitals to obtain pleasure.

Autoeroticism begins in the earliest months of human life when infants begin to explore their own bodies, and their hands reach their genitals in the same way that they reach any other part of the body. This does not mean that infants feel the same sensations that adults do, but they do experience extreme satisfaction on a sensory level. Could it be that masturbation is a natural human act? Yes.

As we experience biological sexual development, our desire for sexual enjoyment also develops full force.

Masturbation as a conscious sexual act begins early in puberty. The individual begins to feel more and more excitement in the game of autoeroticism, until he or she intensifies the practice to the point of experiencing orgasm. One very common misconception is that this practice is basically for teenagers going through puberty or adolescence. This is absolutely not true. Every human being, in different stages of life, feels the need to masturbate, regardless of gender or age. In fact, some people are only capable of reaching maximum pleasure and excitement through masturbation. This can be due to personal issues with intimacy, whether physical or psychological. But even in these cases, it shouldn't be considered an illness or some form of negative or abnormal behavior.

Autoeroticism:
Haven't You Ever Tried It?

Autoeroticism is a valid alternative expression of sexual energy for anyone in a relationship or not. The knowledge, erotic sensitivity and fantasies that each individual gains from exploring his or her body are transferred onto our relationships with others. Masturbation, therefore, amplifies pleasurable experiences of all sorts.

Here I will describe a simple and satisfying method for masturbating without guilt and in a relaxed fashion: Go into a room where you feel calm and secure, certain that nobody will interrupt you. Take off all your clothes and find a mirror. Start by exploring your face; caress your lips and cheeks. Observe how the erotic energy begins to remind you of when you were a baby and you touched yourself with satisfaction and no guilt. Now feel how beautiful your skin feels, and how much you enjoy caressing your own body. Follow the contours of your shoulders, observe and touch your breasts. Caress your nipples tenderly and gently. You can make the whole experience even more sensuous with some massage oil that will nourish your skin. Feel the energy that radiates from your chest, from your heart. Now allow your hands to roam down to the area of your waist, touching yourself wherever it feels best. If you can, stay aware of your mouth, touch your tongue. Now continue caressing yourself, your belly button, your back, your buttocks, hips, thighs, your genitals . . . linger here a little bit, feel every molecule vibrating within your body and the pleasure it inspires. Don't hold back from enjoying every area equally. Explore your intimate parts, feel the heat and smell your own fragrance. Surrender to an orgasm if you really feel ready to do so, then relax and lie there with yourself for a few minutes. Allow all that energy that you've generated to just flow.

The important thing is to surrender to yourself, for you to have loved yourself with the same level of desire and passion that you use to make love to your partner. You are a sensual being. If you didn't feel the energy of your own sexuality and eroticism, try again on another day. Be sure to focus your attention on what you are doing and especially on what you feel. This will help intensify the level of intimacy between you and your partner if you can share this experience with him or her. Invite your partner to do this exercise either alone or alongside you. Later on, talk about your experiences and plan to do the exercise with each of you exploring the other's body as you did your own. Ask your partner: What do you feel? What are your most sensitive areas? What would you like to do afterward? Is there a particular fantasy that you would like to act out? Discuss everything that you've experienced in your sexual relationship, but be sure to avoid remembering your experiences with other partners. Sometimes comparisons can be negative and could hurt your partner's feelings. Sadly, the vast majority of couples don't talk about sex after they make love—their likes and dislikes, their feelings, and so on.

SELF-SEX

Some positive aspects of this erotic practice:

- Masturbation, aside from the physical pleasure that it provides, also alleviates tension and stress.
- By getting to know what you like, you can teach your partner how to please you. This can really help to avoid a lot of frustration, awkwardness and emotional drain.
- It is a way to prepare for the sexual act. Sometimes a man will masturbate before sex in order to prevent early ejaculation and achieve a longer-lasting erection.
- Many couples use masturbation to equalize the differences in rhythm and timing; thus, when one partner comes first, the other can masturbate until reaching orgasm.
- Autoeroticism is an act of rediscovering, exploring and strengthening communication with ourselves. It allows us to learn about sex, our erogenous zones and what we need as individuals. We are unique beings, and this allows us to become experts on our own pleasure.
- Autoeroticism is a means through which we learn to value our own sexual organs and to enjoy our own excitement and orgasm. It is a means to keep our essential erotic energy alive.
- Self-sex is a way to feel sexually independent, and it provides excellent preparation for future sexual relationships.
- In the case of couples who suffer from frigidity or lack of sexual satisfaction, masturbation allows for a form of erotic play that facilitates the ease and freedom of reaching orgasm.
- During the act of masturbation, caressing oneself or one's partner using different aromatic oils helps to increase sensitivity and intensify the response in all of our senses, especially touch and smell.

Discovering Your Own Pleasure

This exercise begins with taking a bath in hot water and a few drops
of essential oil that act as an aphrodisiac. You can try rose, sandal-
wood, lavender or any other type of fragrant oil that you like.

- After the bath, to warm and soften the body, use a natural mois-
  turing skin lotion.
- You may do this exercise in bed or in another place where you
  are comfortable.
- Begin by caressing your entire body, including your face,
  breasts, belly and thighs. Allow these caresses to stimulate and
  excite you.
- Feel the pleasure; don't rush the orgasm. Give yourself time
  without rushing so that you can appreciate each sexual sensation to its fullest intensity.
- For men, it is generally advised to refrain from ejaculation.
  Many schools of Eastern wisdom, such as Tantra, consider masturbation to the point of ejaculation to be a squandering of a
  man's vital energy. Besides, the act of containing and controlling
  your orgasm considerably intensifies your sexual pleasure.
- While the body is becoming excited, relax and breathe deeply
  and steadily, until you feel the orgasmic wave sweep through
  your entire body.
- Tense the muscles in your buttocks to intensify your pleasure.
  Maximize your excitement using positive erotic fantasies to
  develop and empower your mind. Then just concentrate on the
  physical experience.
- Once you reach orgasm, it is important to allow yourself to be
  swept away, to surrender fully to the pleasure, expressing it just
  as you feel it, with no sort of prejudice or taboo to hold you
  back: moan, scream, sigh and feel all of the power and pleasure
  that you experience.

Autoeroticism, the Female Genital Area and Women's Confessions

Historically, in many cultures masturbation was considered a "male thing." Rarely does anyone speak about female masturbation. On the contrary, there's nothing wrong with giving yourself sexual pleasure. It's nothing to be ashamed of, nothing to feel guilty about—in fact, there are plenty of reasons to satisfy yourself this way, even if you don't tell anybody about it. Basically, it's liberating, healthy and fun. Women have a great deal of potential to reach orgasm by means of masturbation, either manually or with vibrators and other toys designed for this purpose. Here, imagination plays a huge role. Remember, though, it is not obligatory that you masturbate; the important thing is how you feel. Ultimately, you decide what you want to do.

It is essential to become familiar with the female anatomy in order to learn how to pleasure every part: the clitoris, the vagina, the vaginal lips and the anus. The genitals have many extremely sensitive nerve endings. When touched in very specific ways in order to achieve climax, enormous pleasure is produced, and of course the sensation is experienced in that part of the brain that controls the libido (the hypothalamus gland). Below I will describe how the female genital area works.

The Outer Lips or Labia Majora: These lips fold over the vagina and are extremely sensitive to touch. You should caress them gently, especially using upward and downward movements. You can enhance stimulation by caressing both inside and outside of the lips. Oral sex can also work on this area. To have the length of the lips licked is very exciting; they darken and swell from increased blood flow during sexual arousal. That's why it's helpful to remember that this area provides a good indication of how aroused the woman is at any given time.

The Inner Lips or Labia Minora: The smaller inner lips of the vagina also have extremely sensitive nerve endings. When the woman is aroused, this area becomes humid and lubricated. This allows for the use of fingertips to caress the lips. Playing with a vibrator or fingers in this area can also be highly stimulating.

The Vaginal Opening: Most of the sexually sensitive nerve endings in the vagina are located within the first five centimeters of its entrance. This area is known as the orgasmic platform. During orgasm, it contracts and relaxes in waves of muscle spasms. The rest of the vagina has a lot of nerve endings, but they are far less sensitive, which means that the size of a man's penis is not relevant to a woman's pleasure. Deeper regions of the vagina are incapable of reacting to stimulation. You may also insert the rounded end of a vibrator gently into the orgasmic platform to increase stimulation.

The Clitoris: The tip of the clitoris is located at the opening to the vagina. From the outside, it is more or less the size of a bean, although the size differs in each woman. The clitoris is located under the skin, but emerges erect during sexual stimulation. It is actually an extremely large organ, with nerves connecting to every region of the female genital area. Although the visible part of the clitoris is very small, clitoral stimulation is vital to a woman's complete sexual fulfillment and is often the most direct way to achieve orgasm. Caressing, kissing, licking and circling the finger with rhythmic strokes on the inner lips and clitoris is extremely stimulating. During stimulation, the clitoris may again retreat inside its fold of skin. This is a very natural part of female stimulation and it happens to protect the clitoris. If it is exposed to too much stimulation at this point, it can become inflamed, painful and uncomfortable. Any vibrator that concentrates on the clitoris stimulates, but especially effective are those that fit on the fingertip or those that are molded to the shape of the vulva.

The G-spot: Some women also achieve deep and intense orgasms by stimulating the G-spot. The easiest way to find it is to lie down with a few pillows under your pelvis so that your vaginal opening is elevated: insert a well-lubricated finger into the vagina and gently curl it behind the rough upper vaginal region. Once the G-spot is stimulated and begins to swell, it generally feels like a small bean, though in some women it may swell to the diameter of a coin.

If you want to reach orgasm, don't press too hard or rub too quickly; go slowly and move your finger back and forth or in a circular motion. In other words, rub around the point, but don't press it directly.

The G-spot can be stimulated by your partner's finger using the "come hither" motion, or with a dildo or penis. The best position for stimulating this spot with the penis is to have the woman sit on top of the man. Many women experience multiple orgasms through this type of stimulation and some ejaculate orgasmic fluid. The orgasm experienced by stimulating the G-spot is generally felt very deeply inside the vagina.

Anal Stimulation: Some women like to have their anus caressed or penetrated during sex or masturbation. The nerve endings there are just as sensitive as those in the genital region. You should practice anal sex very carefully and use plenty of lubrication, as the inside of the anus can easily be scratched or hurt. The woman must guide her partner and determine the intensity of the pleasure and the pain. You can also use, in addition to natural penetration, a vibrator or dildo, oral sex, or a finger to achieve penetration and/or stimulation in this region.

Women's Erotic Confessions

Below are the experiences of three women who have found in masturbation new fuel for their sexual fantasies, better sexual relationships with their partners and a stronger sense of erotic self-awareness as women.

Celia, age twenty-seven: *I have plenty of experience, because I've been using this technique since adolescence and now I like to do it with everything. It's very important to me to be mentally excited or to have a fantasy in order to masturbate. It's also very important to me to be alone. I use the tips of my fingers for real stimulation, but it's better to start with little pats or brushing gently across the general area. Once the excitement increases, I start to stimulate my clitoris, and finally I reach a climax rubbing rapidly over the hood of the clitoris. Usually my legs are open and sometimes I also stimulate my nipples with the other hand.*

Joanne, age thirty-three: *If I'm pressed for time, I use the vibrator on the base of my clitoris, with my legs open. I use my fingers to rub around the base of the clitoris and when I'm getting close to orgasm, I move my fingers in a circular motion around my clit. My legs are always spread open, and I switch hands to avoid getting tired. My other hand is usually caressing my breasts, which is my most erogenous zone. And I move my body a lot when I have an orgasm.*

Mara, age thirty: *I usually masturbate with my finger and touch my breasts with the other hand, but not always. Usually I use a back and forth movement on my vagina, or else I just keep my fingers there for a minute. My legs are wide open, with my knees bent, near my face. Sometimes I wiggle a lot, depending on the intensity of my sensations at that moment.*

I have no regrets. I love to enjoy good sex alone or with my partner. It's very liberating. Sometimes I use a vibrator, but I only like to use it when I'm masturbating. I don't like to use it during sex with my partner because I don't want him to feel bad about it.

Another technique that I use: I cross my legs, push my pelvis against a soft object (a pillow works best) and have a fantasy. This is the tried-and-true method. I enjoy touching myself, but it's not as much fun as

doing this. I hardly move, except when I'm ready to come. When I mas-
turbate, I usually squeeze my legs together or cross them one over the other
and I use a towel, rubbing it against my clit rhythmically until I explode.

The Male Genital Anatomy

Whether it's done quickly or slowly, in one position or another, ado-
lescent male masturbation is accepted as a societal norm. But in fact,
men masturbate well into adulthood, in spite of the myths that their
desire for masturbation wanes when they enter a relationship. For
many men, masturbation is a means of understanding and programming their body's sexual responses. Below is a description of
the male erogenous zones and how the male body works.

The External Male Organs: The penis is the organ used for copula-
tion. Its function is to deliver sperm into the female's vagina during
coitus. It is also an excretory organ, housing the tip of the urethra.
The external male genitals are the penis and the scrotum. The shaft
of the penis contains three cylinders of erectile tissue: the two layers
of corpora cavernous ("cavernous bodies"), which are parallel to
one another, and the spongy layer known as corpus spongiosum,
which is underneath them and contains the urethra. During sexual
excitation, the erectile tissue becomes filled with blood, making the
penis hard and erect. In the adult male, the penis is an average of two
to four inches long and slightly over an inch in diameter when flac-
cid; during erection it can extend to a length of five to eight inches
long and about two inches in diameter. These measurements are not
categorical, however.

The Penis: One might say that the penis is made up of two sections:
a posterior section, the glans or head, and another ventral section.
The ventral part, in a state of flaccidity or rest, is soft and cylindri-
cal and hangs vertically. The glans is covered by a fold of skin called
the foreskin, which is like a hood that can be pulled back, except

in newborn infants, exposing the head of the penis. In some children this foreskin is stripped away shortly after birth during circumcision.

The Glans: The glans is the head of the penis. In uncircumcised males, the glans is covered by the foreskin, which is retractable. It is attached to the glans by a band of tissue located on its inner surface called the frenum. The frenum contains numerous nerve endings, making this area sensitive to and sometimes even irritated by excessive rough handling.

The Scrotum: The scrotum or scrotal sack is the layer of skin that covers the testicles. The scrotal sack is divided in two halves, each corresponding to one testicle and its adjacent structures. The primary function of the scrotum is to control and maintain the natural temperature of the testicles. Under certain circumstances, especially in cold weather, the scrotum's muscular fibers make the entire sack shrink or contract, pulling the testicles closer to the body in order to keep them warm. Under other conditions, in hot weather, or during a state of total relaxation, the scrotum becomes softer and more loose, its surface smooth. The testicles then hang farther from the body and stay cooler. The skin is very sensitive, fine and dark in color, characterized by irrigated transversal folds that enclose a lot of nerve endings. These give it its characteristic level of intense sensitivity.

The Male G-spot or Anal Stimulation of the Prostate: This erogenous zone is also referred to sometimes as the A-spot. The G-spot has been physiologically identified as the prostate gland, which surrounds the urethra at the neck of the bladder. Stimulation of the prostate causes more intense orgasms with greater amounts of seminal ejaculation.

It can be difficult for a man to find this area in his own body, because the only way to actually feel it is by entering the anus. The best position in which to discover it is to lie on your back with your knees bent, insert your finger in your anus and press toward the front. There you will feel the prostate as a firm mass of tissue about the size of a walnut that, when stimulated, produces extremely intense sexual arousal.

Autoeroticism in Men

Usually, men masturbate by wrapping one hand around the base of the penis and stroking it in a rhythmical up-and-down movement. Most men also stimulate the glans. Some reach orgasm by rubbing the glans increasingly faster, while others use more sensitivity, as this movement might cause irritation. The ideal pressure, speed and length of movement varies among individuals.

The rhythm is the most important thing, as it creates sexual tension. You can also caress, massage or hold your testicles at the same time as you rub the area between the testicles and the anus. Applying pressure to the base of the penis increases sensitivity and strengthens the erection. Another way to reach orgasm is to gently caress the testicles until the penis becomes erect and then use only two or three fingers to stroke the base instead of wrapping the whole hand around it.

It can take two to five minutes for a man to reach an orgasm, depending on his level of stress, excitation and energy. Most men stroke their penis more quickly as orgasm approaches. Others hold their testicles or the base of the shaft while they ejaculate. If you want to slow down the process of reaching orgasm, go more slowly and occasionally change or interrupt the rhythm of your movement. The sensation of pleasure will last longer and the orgasm will be more intense, although if you hold your orgasm for too long, the reverse may actually be true.

Once a man reaches orgasm, he will not wish to be touched or stimulated. At this time, the penis and especially the glans, become extremely sensitive.

Use a good lubricant. A lot of men use saliva as lubrication during masturbation so that it feels more like real penetration. But saliva may not be enough. The best thing to use is a moisturizing lotion or cream or a water-based lubricant. These products offer a different sensation, since they allow you to stroke harder using the entire palm of the hand directly on the glans, and they prevent irritation in even the most sensitive men.

Men's Erotic Confessions

Here three men describe their experiences with masturbation. These examples can help ignite your imagination and pleasure.

Marc, age thirty-three: *The most unexpected place I ever masturbated was in the lane where you wait for a highway exit. It was nighttime and I was driving and remembering how this married coworker of mine had seduced me. We had just had a going-away party for her at work and she had attended the party with her husband. At the party, her husband was seated at the next table. I never suspected that she was interested in me, until that night. She had been drinking a bit much and we ended up spending the entire evening teasing one another with comments and glances, with no hope or possibility of anything; at one point, she actually caressed my thigh under the table. I was practically exploding from the excitement.*

On my way home from the party that night, alone of course, I was so horny that I couldn't concentrate on driving my car. I pulled over and leaned back a bit in my seat, playing with myself while cars were speeding by on the highway. Unfortunately, I had the bad luck of having a police car pull over beside me, but he never got out of the car.

"Good evening, is there any problem?" The officer asked, rolling his window down.

"No, nothing at all," I replied. "I was falling asleep with a headache, so I chose to pull over for a minute. I'm feeling better now, though."

And there I was with my pants pulled down to my ankles, leaning back in my seat. Luckily, he couldn't see below my chest.

"Okay, drive carefully, good night," he said and left.

Mario, age twenty-five: *I don't masturbate. I make love to myself almost every day when I take a shower. I start out by having a hot fantasy, usually about my ex-girlfriends, and I play with myself until I ejaculate. Even though I live with a woman now, I still feel that it's a release I need before starting my day.*

Peter, age twenty-four: *When I was a teenager, I masturbated anytime, anyplace. Sometimes I'd feel the need to do it and I'd go into the first public restroom I could find. Later I started to repress my need, because a lot of people were saying a lot of negative things about it. This repression caused me a lot of problems in my early relationships. I had to get professional help because I was suffering from premature ejaculation. Later I started masturbating before having sex with my partner, and it helped me to hold an erection. At the same time I discovered that I needed to masturbate in order to have a normal sexual relationship, and I realized that it was all that negative stuff about masturbation that had caused me to have a sexual block.*

Myths about Masturbation

What follows are myths about masturbation. These negative beliefs have become rooted in many people's minds, but it is important to remember that they are untrue:

- Masturbation is a childish form of sexual expression and should be abandoned once we mature.
- It is a poor substitute for "real" sex.
- It's compulsive behavior. Once you start you can't stop.
- The desire to masturbate disappears once you're in a relationship.
- It is physically, mentally and emotionally harmful.
- The orgasms that you experience during masturbation are inferior to those that are produced by sex with a partner.
- Masturbation is a private matter, to be done only in solitude and not to be shared.

- Sex is something you give to others; therefore masturbation is selfish and self-indulgent.
- Only people who are depraved, isolated, lonely or inadequate masturbate.
- Men masturbate but women don't feel any desire or need for it.
- When you get used to orgasms produced during masturbation, you won't be able to reach an orgasm when you're with a partner.

It is important to eliminate these false beliefs from your mind. Masturbation helps you fulfill your erotic needs and allows you to know yourself better sexually, thus nurturing a more satisfying sexual relationship with your partner.

CHAPTER 18

I Love You and
I Want to Arouse You
through Touch

A sexual relationship starts with a tender caress in which the first physical contact is awakened, the senses soar and sensations ignite into a volcano of endless passion.

Erotic Massage for Women and Stimulation of the G-Spot

Massage is an excellent way to awaken sexual energy or to wipe out barriers of shame. It is a great way to become aroused, create an intimate space and get to know your partner's body. It also provides an opportunity to concentrate exclusively on either giving or receiving pleasure.

The best way to discover a woman's sexual needs is to ask her to guide you with her hand and to show you what she likes best. When you begin to massage her, don't concentrate only on her genitals. Remember to caress her breasts and thighs—they are highly erogenous zones as well. For an erotic massage to be effective, it's important to observe the receiver's reactions. Deepen or modify the stimuli accordingly.

Women can reach orgasm by stimulation of either the G-spot or the clitoris. Most women characterize clitoral orgasm as more intense and G-spot orgasm as deeper. Discovering the female G-spot during erotic massage is very important. That area is extremely sensitive and will generally produce intense orgasms when properly stimulated. Once you become familiar with this point through massage, it will be easier to find during penetration. Here are the steps to follow:

When you begin to caress and masturbate your partner, it is important that you lubricate your hands first. Explore the inner and outer lips with your fingers. Gently perceive how it feels when you touch her, continuing with very delicate movements and always trying to stimulate other erogenous zones. Touch her breasts, kiss her neck and caress her sensitive inner thighs. With your index finger, try to caress the clitoris in a rhythmic manner, always keeping a steady and gentle motion. Caress her vagina gently with your other hand, making sure your fingers are well-lubricated. You can use any variety of linear or circular movements with your finger but always in a delicate and steady rhythm. You can also use her hand to guide you. If she has a spot that she likes having caressed and also enjoys oral sex, you can use both methods. Stimulate the clitoris or the vagina with your tongue and use the finger to keep penetrating the vagina.

Insert a finger gently and deeply into the vagina, and once she is ready and lubricated, follow with a second finger. Place your index finger on her anus. Don't insert it. Instead, press gently while moving your finger around. If she asks you to, you can penetrate her, but generally it is best to keep vaginal play separate from anal play. Now place the palm of your hand on her mons pubis (pubic area) and start moving your hand in a circular motion. Repeat these movements until she reaches her orgasm. Lift your fingers and gently caress the vaginal lips using a steady, rhythmic motion. An excellent way to learn how she enjoys receiving pleasure is to place your fingers on top of hers while she masturbates. Especially take note of the rhythm that she needs to climax.

To find her G-spot, insert your index finger in her vagina, cover the clitoris with your hand and let your fingers rest on her mons pubis. Alternate the stimulation between the internal G-spot (at the roof of the vagina), the clitoris and the external G-spot (above the bladder). Press firmly on the G-spot as though you were pressing a doorbell. Then continue pressing and releasing to increase her pleasure. It's common for women to want to be penetrated at that point. One of the advantages of stimulating the G-spot is that many women who receive this form of stimulation affirm that they enjoy multiple orgasms and that their orgasms are more intense and last longer.

Massage as a Means to Male Multiple Orgasms

Make sure to use lubricant on your hands to avoid irritating the penis. If the man is not circumcised, take the penis and, with one hand, pull the skin back toward the base of the shaft and cover the skin with your fingers to keep the skin pulled taut. Using your other hand move the penis rhythmically, pressing gently to stimulate the organ until erect. Immediately rub the penis between the palms of your hands, as though you were rubbing a stick to make a fire. The man may or may not reach ejaculation via this massage, but if he does, he will feel an explosion of pleasure.

Unblocking energy: Wrap your hand around the head of the penis and rotate your hand as if you were trying to unlock a door. As always, your hands must be very well lubricated. Now rotate gently toward the other side, slowly repeating this movement from one side to the other. This massage unblocks erection problems and also improves blood circulation in the penis, allowing for greater physical flexibility. Do not apply extreme pressure during this massage.

Closed-fist multiple orgasms: Take the penis and wrap your hand around it in the shape of a fist, allowing the penis to penetrate the opening in the hand. With your well-lubricated hand, rotate the fist gently from side to side. Before the head of the penis peeks out from inside the fist, cover it. It will feel as though the penis is penetrating deeper and deeper into a vagina. He will experience indescribable pleasure if, in addition to this, you caress his testicles delicately, using gentle movements from the anus toward the penis. This type of massage will enable the man to reach sustained or multiple orgasms.

The Male G-spot or A-spot: Recent discoveries show that men also possess strategic zones of heightened or extreme sensitivity that, when explored, may be stimulated in order to unleash orgasms of extraordinary dimensions. Some refer to it as the male G-spot, while others call it the A-spot. As I mentioned earlier in the section on male erogenous zones, this point is located at the site of the prostate. You can feel the walnut shape of the prostate if you gently introduce a finger into the anus and guide it toward the front wall of the rectum. At a depth of approximately one to three inches, press toward the front (toward the penis) and you will feel the small bump there. The position that best facilitates this activity is to have him lying face up with his knees against his chest. It will be even more exciting for him if his partner is the one to initiate the exploration. Using a gentle, slow motion, and with the hand fully lubricated, massage him until he reaches orgasm, which will be more intense than usual.

Tips for avoiding pain:
- Prevent scratches and cuts by keeping your nails neatly trimmed.
- Use latex gloves or a condom for maximum protection.
- Apply plenty of lubricant onto the finger.

Before introducing the finger, gently touch the outer part of the anus using a circular movement. Introduce the tip of the finger into the anal canal to a depth of about a half inch and twist it gently, as though you were drawing tiny circles inside him.

It is important that you continuously ask the man if he is feeling pleasure and do not explore any further if he decides not to continue.

Mutual Masturbation

Mutual masturbation is a very beneficial form of preparing for coitus. It consists of reciprocal stimulation of the genitals in order to produce pleasure and sexual arousal in both partners. By way of these caresses you will discover the intimate details of your lover's body. You will also be able to freely express your desires and preferences by letting your partner know what you like most and where. During this sexual practice, it's important to establish clear communication. There are many preferences, and even the same person may desire different types of stimulation depending on the occasion. By taking advantage of your hands, it's possible to move with great precision, allowing both partners to enjoy the most sublime of sensations.

Fabian, age twenty-four: *I met my girlfriend a few weeks ago and since we live in different states, we've decided to start having phone sex. She loves it and we do it five or six times a week. She recently started using a vibrator and I love it when I hear her have an orgasm. It's really hot. She imagines my penis in her vagina and I imagine myself inside of her while I masturbate. It's the moment of climax for both of us. If your partner's far away and you have the opportunity to try this, I'm sure you'll be pleasantly surprised.*

Pablo, age thirty-three: *My wife and I love to masturbate. It's given me absolute confidence in myself and in my sexuality. My wife and I started to get into mutual masturbation after five years of marriage and it's given us unique results. We lie down next to each other and we start touching each other slowly. She stimulates me with her left hand while I caress her clitoris with the middle finger of my right hand. I get excited right away, anticipating our mutual masturbation session. Our breathing gets stronger, she starts moving her hips to keep up with my strokes, holding my penis in her hand. Soon she slides her hand down between her legs, opening her lips, touching her clitoris. She guides my hand to her breast, to her nipple. Her finger moves in circles around her clitoris, rubbing harder and harder. She slides one finger inside her lips. Then she goes back to her clitoris, touching her right side, her sensitive side. She continues to stimulate me with her left hand; I grow wild with excitement, just knowing she's touching herself. I put my right arm under her, reach over and caress her nipples. Her nipples get big and hard when she gets excited. I have to be really careful, stopping from time to time, so she can reach a climax just from me stimulating her nipples. Her hips start pushing her vulva upward wanting her fingers. She moans and moves uncontrollably. I'm about to climax. She's increased her stimulation of my penis and her fingers are squeezing me harder. It's hard for me to hold back my orgasm. Her legs are wide open; she's pushing her fingers deeply inside her lips, reaching her G-spot. She uses her index finger to rub her clitoris while her fingers move in and out of her vulva. Now she's moaning loudly, screaming from excitement. She's starting to reach her climax. Knowing that she's in the process of reaching her orgasm makes me relax and I feel myself reaching climax as well. I can't hold back any longer, my penis is throbbing and I'm ejaculating. Now she's moving her hand up and down so fast that my ejaculation is all over both of us. My body starts to jerk as though it's having convulsions. At that moment, she's in the throes of her orgasm, moaning; her hips push furiously upward trying to force her fingers deeper inside her lips. Her orgasm seems to last forever. After she comes, she rests her head on my shoulder and we both fall asleep.*

Guide your partner with your own movements. This is the best way to communicate your desires and greatest pleasures. Another way to learn how to massage your partner is to pay close attention to his or her gestures, indications, movements and signs of pleasure.

CHAPTER 19

I Love You and
I Want to Kiss You All Over

The taste of you makes my mouth water.
I feel myself drowning in your white honey while you thrust and
moan with ecstasy.
I won't pull my lips from your sex until you explode and feel all
the magic of my tongue and my wet lips.
I want to see you sweetly overcome with pleasure, body and
soul.

Oral Sex:
Pleasure and Taste

Remember that our bodies experience pleasure through sensations on our skin in a sensual and extraordinary manner, and the skin's varied folds and flavors may be explored delightfully using the mouth. These tastes and textures are marvelously diverse in both men's and women's bodies.

In this chapter we will explore oral sex, which is a very gratifying practice between couples. Cunnilingus (oral sex to satisfy a woman) and fellatio (oral sex to satisfy a man) are habitual practices among same-sex as well as heterosexual couples. Oral sex can be performed any number of ways, but it always involves using the mouth to give one's partner pleasure.

Oral Pleasure for Women

Cunnilingus is a technique that you can learn and perfect by following certain steps to enjoy the benefits. Women and men take their pleasure in a unique manner depending on physical and psychological factors. There is no limit to the levels of play that are possible when it comes to exploring all the possibilities of sex. Oral sex arouses pleasure that is truly exquisite, especially when performed with finesse, awareness and love. This technique can take place before or after coitus, but I recommend using it during foreplay.

Positions

Because oral sex can take awhile, it's best to find a comfortable position for both partners. When a woman is receiving, it is best for her to lie back with her legs elevated. She can also kneel over her partner's face as he lies on his back, placing her vulva onto his mouth. In that position, she can enjoy looking at her partner's face. The person performing cunnilingus can lie on top of a pillow in order to raise his head up to the level of his partner's vulva. The woman can also place a pillow under her hips to elevate them to the level of her lover's mouth.

Igniting the Desire for Oral Sex

Start by gliding your tongue down her chest, moving slowly down to her belly, and then use your tongue and lips gently on her legs and knees, caressing and holding the inner part of her thighs. Switch from one leg to the other, licking the area around her thighs over and over again. Keep going, slowly; you'll begin to notice the degree of desire that your partner feels. At that point, bring your tongue close to the area around her pubis.

Don't Forget to Stimulate

While performing oral sex, don't stop caressing her breasts with well-lubricated fingers. Touch her belly and all the parts of her body that you can reach. Each woman will react differently and have her own specific preferences. As you move your tongue and hands to different areas ask her if she likes being stimulated in the spot that you're touching. It's important to know what she likes, how she wants to be caressed or licked: does she want it sweeter, deeper, steadier, harder?

Pressure, Rhythm and Tongue

There are women who prefer the tongue to be rigid and firm, those who want the oral massage to be soft and slow, while others like a hard and fast approach. There is one important rule to keep in mind while performing oral sex: you have to maintain a steady rhythm once you've found her clitoris. Otherwise, the woman may lose her concentration. For many women, it is bothersome when her partner changes rhythms, especially if she's getting close to orgasm.

Tune in to Her Wishes

Before you lick her clitoris, try moving your tongue around her vulva every possible way you can dream of. Discover her clitoris by accident. Caress, kiss and lick the inner part of her thighs. Lick softly around the area where her vulva and thighs meet. Glide your tongue gently along her pubic mound and the outer lips of her vagina. It's important to take your time with each area, so you can tell how your lover is reacting. Little by little, using a slow steady rhythm, slide your tongue along her outer and inner lips. When the woman wants to direct her own pleasure, she can use verbal instructions, sounds, hand gestures, or she can move her body. She'll take her lover's head in her hands and guide his mouth to the place she loves best. The partner must be open to this possibility, and not think that he knows more than she does. A lot of women fear losing their partners by being too demanding in bed. That's why it is so important to talk openly before and after sex to clear up one another's needs.

How to Avoid Getting Tired

Many people get tired while performing oral sex. That's why it's important to make sure your jaw is relaxed. Keep your mouth half open to avoid biting your partner. You shouldn't extend your tongue fully. It's best to keep your mouth close to the clitoris; when you feel like you are getting tired, you can continue the rhythm with your hand and then start again with your tongue. The hand must always be totally lubricated, either with saliva or with a lubricant that won't change the flavor of her secretions.

Penetration with the Tongue

The woman may enjoy having you insert your tongue into her vagina, stimulating the vaginal walls. It's not necessary to insert your tongue very deeply. Usually the most sensitive tissue is close to the entrance. Place your tongue at the entrance of her vagina and then use it to penetrate her. Use your hands to softly separate the outer lips to achieve better penetration. Continue to use your fingers to stimulate her clitoris. When she appears to be ready for orgasm, use your lubricated fingers to slide back the hood that covers her clitoris and lick it. It is exquisitely sensitive at this moment and she will experience a profound orgasm.

Odors and Flavors

If the woman feels that her genitals smell or taste bad, she should ask her partner what he thinks. Her partner may actually enjoy the very smell that she finds unappealing. But before making love, it's always recommended that you take a shower together so that both partners feel comfortable. Or take a relaxing bath to help stimulate the sexual relationship. Perhaps the best way for the woman to accept and know her own normal and healthy vaginal odor and flavor is to sniff and taste her fingers during masturbation. Bear in mind that a woman's vaginal secretions change during her menstrual cycle. Her level of sexual arousal may be more intense at different times of the month, and the odor and flavor of her vagina may change; these factors may also be affected by her diet. Many oils, creams, lubricants and personal hygiene products are specifically designed to add fragrance and flavor to this area of women's bodies.

Shaved and Chic

A lot of couples find that the practice of trimming or shaving the woman's pubic hair makes cunnilingus easier. Some women find cunnilingus more pleasant and personal hygiene easier when they are completely shaved, while some couples feel quite the opposite and consider it much sexier to have all of the pubic hair covering the female genitalia. Shaving or trimming the pubic hair is a matter of personal choice; it is not in any way a requirement for oral sex.

The Signs of Satisfaction in a Woman

Women should be honest with their partners and never fake pleasure or orgasm. In spite of this, a lot of men remain in doubt and ask me how they can be sure if their partner is enjoying herself. Here are a few signs to watch for:

- As she's becoming excited, the woman's body extends itself and her eyes close.
- If she ardently wishes to be satisfied, she may sweat abundantly.
- If she feels an orgasm coming, she squeezes the walls of her vagina as tightly as possible.
- As the orgasm approaches, she may look intently into her partner's eyes.
- She may pant and be unable to control the tone of her voice.
- Her nostrils may dilate and her mouth may be half-open.
- Her ears and face may become reddened and the tip of her tongue may be slightly pointed.
- Her hands may feel as though they are on fire, her belly may feel hot and she may murmur unintelligible words.
- Her saliva may flow copiously under her tongue and her body may cling to the man's body.
- The pulse in her vulva may be easily perceived and her vagina may feel extremely wet.
- If her desire has been placated, her body may extend itself and her eyes may remain closed as though she were asleep.
- Her body may appear as though she is dead and her limbs may hang limply.
- If the woman is longing for penetration, her breathing pattern may change and she may clamor to embrace her partner's body.

More Erotic Confessions

Lila, age thirty-four: *I love oral sex! Yes, I do, and I'll tell the whole world about it. The most divine thing for me is discovering how my partner does it differently each time, feeling the warmth of his breath getting closer to my sex, to my center; the skill of his hands and fingers, his rhythm, the way he plays with his tongue. I love how his thick lips take in the different folds and how he makes it so that he can entertain me and also watch me. I love seeing his face while I'm enjoying myself.*

Amanda, age forty-three: *Oral sex is a sensual and delicate sensation. When he sticks his tongue in me, it gives me tremendous pleasure. But when he runs his tongue along the space between my breasts and he finds my nipple, I feel a total current of passion running through me. I feel ecstasy.*

The sensation of pleasure in my breasts is ample and infinite, just as female sexuality is ample and infinite in depth. I have girlfriends who have told me that their sexual desire is kindled by the mere brush of their nipple; I am one of them. It makes me hot to feel my lover's lips approaching my breasts and my pelvis.

Albert, age forty-five: *As a man I've had lots of experience with oral sex, but I remember that one of my partners had a clitoris that was so sensitive it was hard to touch her there without causing pain. One good tip that I learned, as far as giving a woman oral pleasure when she has a really sensitive clitoris, is to relax the tongue. A lot of guys make the mistake of keeping their tongue muscles rigid and licking the clitoris with the tip of the tongue as soon as they start having sex. Keep your tongue flat, lick her thighs and her pubic area, and that relaxes the woman. Another thing I found is that a woman with a very sensitive clitoris needs to feel love and support before making love. If the woman feels secure and loved, her body will probably respond better to lovemaking.*

Fellatio:
Oral Pleasure for Men

There are many different ways to give a man pleasure with your mouth. Below are some examples:

Direct: The woman takes the base of the penis and places it all the way back into her mouth, squeezing it firmly with her lips. While sucking on him, she stretches the penis out of her mouth, keeping up the pressure with her lips. She continues to take the penis back into her mouth, each time opening her mouth wider to facilitate more penetration, repeating this act over and over until the man reaches orgasm.

Bites: Taking the penis into her well-lubricated fingers and grabbing its base like an ice-cream cone, she delicately uses her lips and teeth and bites up and down the sides of the penis.

Kissing: Another technique of oral sex is the kiss. The woman holds the penis in her hand and covers it with kisses sprinkled with bites while gently sliding her tongue up and down the shaft. It is important to let the man guide you with his hands and let you know where he most loves to be kissed.

Total Suction: The woman introduces the whole penis into her mouth (including the testicles), squeezing it against her throat as though she were swallowing him whole. The woman may also move her hands in a back and forth motion up and down the shaft of the penis. She can also use one of her hands to caress the testicles and the anal area.

Some women don't care for oral sex—so much so that they won't go anywhere near the area. This is often caused by too much pubic hair in that region. If this is the case, the couple may decide to have the man carefully shave his pubic area.

The Taste of Semen

It's very important that both members of a couple know their own erotic preferences as well as one another's. It's also advisable to make a few rules about lovemaking. For example, not all women enjoy swallowing or sucking the man's semen. If the woman feels no desire to do so, the couple should agree upon a way to signal that the woman should remove his penis from her mouth in time to avoid this.

The flavor of a man's semen depends in large part on his diet. A diet of fish and meat produces a very sour taste. Avoid performing fellatio after a man has eaten asparagus, as this can produce a very bitter flavor. Scientific studies have shown that men who consume lots of honey and natural non-citrus fruit juices produce semen that tastes sweet. There are also certain dietary supplements that men can take to change the flavor of their semen. The companies that create and market these products claim that the salty flavor of human semen can be altered to taste like apple, orange or strawberry. You may also want to try consuming ginger. In addition to being used for centuries as an aphrodisiac, it has also been said to benefit fertility by increasing the volume and mobility of sperm. Other substances that affect the flavor of a man's semen include alcohol, caffeine, cocaine, marijuana and nicotine. All of these give semen an acrid and bitter flavor. Semen isn't only affected by diet. It also changes depending on personal hygiene. It's not news to anyone that semen contains traces of urine and preseminal fluids that mix together during ejaculation.

Some men like the flavor of their own semen and like to use it as a stimulus. They smear their semen all over their partner's breasts and other erogenous zones and then lick it up.

Odors, Flavors and Colors

Women aren't the only ones who can be provocative. Men too can use scented and flavored sexual creams and oils on their buttocks and testicles in order to soften their skin and enhance oral sex. Certain aromatic oils, such as lavender and almond, may be used during the sexual act to stimulate semen production. These oils contain odors and flavors that stimulate the flow of blood to the penis and thus strengthen the erection and improve the semen's quality.

Secret Recipe: Prepare a delightful sex cream with honey, cinnamon, apple juice and chocolate. This will provide you with delicious oral experiences.

Colorful Sex: For women who love oral sex, flavored lipstick can be worn while practicing this technique. You can rub semen on your lips and kiss your partner's whole body, tracing designs with your lips. Use different-colored lipsticks. This playful fun can become a new fantasy.

The most important thing in these cases is for both partners to express their natural tendencies, feelings, creativity and desire, leaving behind rational thinking and respecting one another's likes and dislikes.

Addicted to Semen

I've had several interesting experiences during my conferences and video chats, but one that comes to mind involved a woman who claimed that she had a perfect technique that made her partner get two erections and have two ejaculations in twenty minutes. Her name was Sara, she was around thirty-one years old and she swore that her technique was 100 percent effective.

First I lick his penis while looking seductively into his eyes. I kiss the tip over and over again, until I have his entire penis in my mouth. I go up and down, rubbing my teeth against the sides. Little by little, I swallow the semen. I swallow it all. Of course my partner has reached orgasm, but I don't let him rest. I lick the penis again very intensely, change my rhythm, pull it out of my mouth entirely and lick the tip again. Then I suck his whole penis again. He spills more semen into my mouth, like thick warm milk. I lick the delicious flavor of semen; it's like sweet and sour with a mineral taste. I lick the semen off his belly until not a drop is left. Without waiting, I stimulate his testicles with my mouth, and I lick his anus. This way I can drink his semen a thousand and one times.

Every man's semen tastes different, but none of my partners have ever turned down this ritual. I've tried every possible flavor of semen and now I think I've gotten addicted to it. In fact, I don't think I can reach an orgasm without tasting his semen first.

No Mint, Please

Among the many e-mails that I receive daily, one in particular stands out. The woman, who did not identify herself, said that she hated oral sex but that her partner would force her to do it to him. One day she decided to try covering his penis with her favorite ice cream: mint chocolate chip. She totally enjoyed oral sex that time. Her partner got so excited that he penetrated her wildly at that moment. The mint irritated the inside of her vagina and she had to make a quick escape to rinse out the irritating itch. When she visited her gynecologist, she was embarrassed about having to explain the cause of her irritation.

Men are typically more bashful when talking about oral sex, but many of them do comment that aside from having their partner concentrate on their penis and testicles, what really turns them on is when their partner stimulates their G-spot in the anal zone (described in chapter 12).

Mutual Oral Sex:
The World-Famous Sixty-nine Position

The position for mutual oral sex is known throughout the world as sixty-nine (as the two numbers—69—are inverted like two human bodies). Sixty-nine is one of the most popular positions for enjoying oral sex. It is done by inverting the partners' two bodies so that while the man is sucking on the woman's clitoris, the woman can be sucking on the man's penis while stimulating his testicles.

During this practice, all of the tips for mutual masturbation and oral sex are applicable. The sixty-nine position is generally appropriate after both partners feel totally comfortable in the relationship. Usually this position is carried out while each partner is lying down; however there are those who opt for vertical variations. One of the partners stands and supports the other partner while both stimulate the other's genitals. The person being supported is in an upside-down position. In heterosexual couples, the man usually supports the woman, while in homosexual couples the balance is determined by each partner's size and weight. There are also those who enjoy doing this in front of a mirror in order to excite each other even further.

Oral sex is a delicate technique; it requires concentration and learning. Once you have both mastered it, the relationship is assured many hours of immense and scintillating erotic pleasure.

CHAPTER 20

I Love You and
I Want to Explore Every
Part of You

You began gently running your hands all over my body, wanting to discover me. First you caressed my back, my waist, and then you slid your hands down my thighs, all the while kissing my buttocks. I watched you exploring me and was thrilled to see the look of tenderness in your eyes while you took pleasure in my body. In one magical second, the two of us ignited into a flame of passion and we made love in a way that we had never experienced before.

Anal Sex

Anal coitus is the introduction of the penis or different accessories or sex toys into the rectum. This produces a great deal of pleasure for both men and women. Anal sex used to be considered "unnatural," yet this practice was long used (mistakenly) to preserve virginity and to avoid unwanted pregnancy. Today, the term *unnatural* is outdated, and the act is recognized as a natural and enjoyable part of sex.

The anus is a sphincter muscle and, in contrast to the vagina, does not lubricate itself; however, it is very similar to the vagina in that it too houses many sensitive nerve endings that produce an

205

immense amount of sexual pleasure and/or pain if not carried out correctly. The anus is a narrow ring whose function is to eliminate bodily waste. The rectal tissue is very fine and delicate. It can tear easily, breaking blood vessels and releasing a plethora of microbes, bacteria and viruses that can spread transmissible diseases such as AIDS. This is why it is extremely important to prevent contact between blood and sexual fluids. Always use a condom during anal penetration.

Anal Techniques

The most important thing necessary to enjoy anal sex is patience and care. And the desire to participate in anal sex must be mutual.

- Before anal penetration, there must be a good preexisting physical relationship. Wash the anal area well. You can use a warm water enema to clean out the internal walls. It's also wise to use condoms, as the rectum contains bacteria that can cause urethal infections. Change the condom before switching to vaginal penetration, as these same bacteria can cause vaginal infections as well.
- Be sure to use plenty of lubrication and to stimulate the anus with your finger before introducing the penis. This is important because the person being penetrated has to be totally aroused.
- Begin by gently sliding one finger very slowly into the anus, allowing your partner to get used to the sensation. Then pull the finger out and introduce it again. This activity may take place before anal sex in order to help the person feel more comfortable, and it might even be wise to wait a few days to see if the person really does desire anal penetration.
- Use a good lubricant at all times during anal penetration.
- I want to reiterate the importance of using condoms. Anal sex can spread harmful microorganisms that the body normally rids itself of through this region.

The initial penetration is always the most difficult part. Perform anal penetration carefully, gently and slowly. You must stop if your partner feels intense pain that is intolerable or if he or she expresses very strong resistance or simply doesn't like it.

It is best not to move on to vaginal coitus immediately after performing anal coitus. You must take hygienic measures such as washing the penis (and/or the finger that was used for anal penetration). It is also necessary to change to a fresh condom to prevent the risk of transferring bacteria from the rectum into the vagina.

Eight Perfect Positions for Anal Sex

There are many positions that are wonderful for anal sex. Below are a few examples:

The Active Posture: In this position, the woman is on top. This allows her to regulate the rate of penetration. While he is gently penetrating her anus, he should caress her clitoris and introduce the fingers of his other hand into her vagina, feeling his penis penetrating the adjacent orifice. The alternate movements between the man's hands and his penis will unleash an uncontrollable orgasm in the woman.

The Creative Posture: He stretches out on his back with his legs open in a forty-five-degree angle, lying passively. She initiates a slow seductive dance and stands naked above his head, offering him a full view of her genitals. She slides downward with her legs open until she is positioned vertically above his erect penis. He provokes her by grabbing her ankles and caressing her legs. She begins to lower herself slowly until she is resting her knees on either side of him and sitting on her partner's pubic area. Her lover uses one finger to slowly stimulate her anus using circular movements, while using his other hand to fetch saliva for lubrication. After caressing each other in this way, she rises slowly and invites him to penetrate her. He responds by pressing his glans against her orifice, but it is the woman who sets the rhythm by slowly rising and descending on her knees while masturbating with her other hand. Her partner maintains the tension by alternating gentle caresses with tiny scratches on his lover's legs, thighs and buttocks.

The Tamed Posture: He supports himself against a table, takes his partner by the hips and draws her closer and closer to his penis with her back toward him. The man must make himself comfortable enough to make love and the woman can support herself by leaning against her partner's pelvis. The woman may be penetrated anally at that moment, while leaning forward as far as her flexibility allows. This posture is recommended for when the woman is well lubricated, since it allows for very deep penetration.

Temptation: In order to achieve greater intimacy, you may choose a place in which it is easy to feel uninhibited, such as the bathroom, especially after enjoying a stimulating bath, shower or sauna together. She is standing with her back to her partner, supporting herself against a towel rack or some other solid fixture on the wall bending forward to almost a ninety-degree angle. Her buttocks become an offering of pleasure for her lover. Her skin, humid with the heat of passion mingled with steam in the air showcases the wetness of her sex, which glistens with undeniable proof of desire.

While she stands sturdily on her feet and opens her legs, he grabs her buttocks with both of his hands. In this posture, which unleashes both partners' animal instincts, he has control of the position and decides the moment of penetration, but she does not have to settle for a totally passive role. Using slow movements, she can press herself against him and set her own rhythm.

Total Possession: She lies facedown and stretched out with her legs partially closed. He observes her while standing, kneels slowly and lies facedown on top of her. The weight of his body and the heat of the two bodies pressed together make this contact very intimate and extremely arousing. The growing erection becomes locked between the woman's legs, where the opening is just barely enough for him to rub his penis against her in a preliminary form of masturbation. The passion continues: she reaches one of her arms back to feel his tight legs, while he passionately kisses her neck, sucking and licking her earlobes. Then, sliding his hand around to the front of her body, he starts slowly masturbating her. She can guess where his other hand will end up as it slides down her back. When the temperature reaches its highest point, and once he notices that her sphincter muscle is relaxed, he firmly spreads her buttocks open and gently introduces his penis inside of her. She instinctively presses her hips up toward him and he descends with fury until the two are melted together and the penetration becomes deeper with every thrust.

The Elixir: The man abundantly lubricates his fingers, as well as his partner's anus, introducing first one finger and then a second inside of her. He then sits on the bed with his legs extended before him, preferably leaning against a wall. She begins to slowly sit on him with her back to him. While she sits on his legs, she allows him to penetrate her anal region gently, after having been sufficiently aroused and lubricated. In this position, he can caress her breasts, kiss her neck and also stimulate her clitoris.

The Two Pillars: The couple is standing leaning against a wall, or with the woman leaning against a bed or table, with the man positioned behind the woman. She can spread her legs or keep them closer together while he penetrates her. The penetration will be more or less deep, depending on how far apart her legs are. The contact between the two lovers will be very intense, allowing him to touch and masturbate his partner. The movement can be controlled by both partners, with either or both setting the rhythm. It can be done totally while standing.

The Spoon: This posture allows the partners to have sex for long periods without getting tired, and is one of the most comfortable positions for both partners. The couple lies down sideways, one behind the other, intertwining their legs while opening them. In this case, penetration is not as deep as it can be in other positions, thus making the position recommendable for those who have never experienced anal sex. It is also a good position to initiate the sexual act. The man can also reach the woman's clitoris in this position, making it possible for him to masturbate her during penetration. If they want to change the position, they can roll over while he is still inside of her, until the woman is on her belly with the man on top of her.

Confessions

Jack, age forty: *I practiced anal sex with my partner. The position we chose was the creative posture and I reached the most incredible orgasm I could ever imagine. All the muscles in her body started shaking, as though her body was totally electrified. I felt these uncontrollable waves of energy and ecstasy. It was hard for me to control my ejaculation, but I tried. Her muscles were trembling uncontrollably under her skin all over her body and her voice sounded like a deep groan that was coming out of me. I felt every one of her movements, every breath. And it was like that until I spilled every last drop of my sperm, and I must confess I had never been so aroused in my life. Afterwards, the waves of pleasure calmed down some, then our voices quieted and finally we found ourselves lying in silence and peace, pleasure and—for me— total amazement.*

Kristi, age thirty-two: *I am personally very turned on by anal sex. But at first my partner had to have a lot of patience with me. He spent a lot of time on the preliminaries before getting to the actual act of anal sex, much more than he did before the first time we had vaginal sex. He started with his fingers, but he also used his mouth (the anus must be very clean for this, otherwise this isn't very pleasant). Thanks to his perseverance and tenderness, I reached new heights of pleasure that were much more intense than usual, because he had prepared me to be more receptive and aroused, which helped to ease the pain and mitigate all my initial fears.*

It is important to learn sexual techniques and practice them in a way that will bring you to perfect satisfaction. Love is the most important area of our lives, and we all deserve to experience total sexual enjoyment.

CHAPTER 21

I Love You and
You Fuel My Fantasies

I didn't know you while I was fantasizing about you.
I imagined your heavenly eyes observing my body,
But you were a stranger to me.
I felt your rose-colored mouth drenched with passion,
But I didn't know if you desired me as I did you.
Now that my fantasy is a reality, all I want is your arms
To protect me for all of eternity.

Fantasies and Eroticism

Why do we hide our sexual fantasies? What represses us? What prevents you from accepting your own fantasies? Would you like to know them and free them? Would you like to know and manage your lover's fantasies? The answers to these and other questions will be revealed in this chapter.

A fantasy corresponds to a mental representation of something that we have lived through or simply that we create in our minds. It can also be compared to an inner movie that we imagine in the most convincing way. The imagination is the greatest aphrodisiac there is. That is why indulging in sexual fantasies is an erotic pastime that provokes sexual excitement. Sexual fantasies are not deviations; they are useful allies in healthy and satisfying sexual relationships. Shared erotic fantasies enrich a couple's relationship and can revitalize their sex life.

Not all erotic fantasies must be acted out. Their most effective function is to infuse mental erotic stimulation into the relationship. The majority of fantasies involve situations or sexual activities that the person has never actually experienced, and that generally are not going to be acted out. They are merely positive and inoffensive daydreams, becoming problematic only when they interfere with an individual's habitual conduct or they become the only source of sexual stimulation for either partner.

Some people worry about the content of their fantasies and feel guilty about imagining certain things. They may fear that those thoughts imply that they would really behave that way. Given that a lot of life's conflicts are caused by forbidden behaviors, many people feel that they have some kind of psychological problem or personality flaw. In fact, in the vast majority of cases, this is not true. In general, sexual fantasies are merely a quest for pleasure ignited by the imagination.

Fantasies: The Dark Side

Human beings have an inner and outer world. The inner world is the playground of ideas, thoughts, experiences and feelings. The outer world houses all that is perceived by our five senses. Between these two spaces exists an area of fantasy that has nothing to do with specific perceptions regarding the outer world. Based on this logic, we can affirm that a sexual fantasy is a reproduction of images based on lived or desired experiences, but they do not necessarily provoke us to experience it in the outer world. We may simply allow ourselves to feel them, express them and/or think about them. During one of my conferences I clearly recall one man who told to me that he had acted out his wife's fantasy, and that it was "pretty special." His wife's fantasy was to have sex with several men at once. He found seven men who all had sex with his wife at the same time while he watched.

He asked me if there was any possibility that his wife had been spiritually or psychologically damaged by the act. He mentioned that she seemed depressed and showed no sexual interest whatsoever. Some people perform acts without regard for how they will affect them. Some things are safe to bring to life but others are meant to remain in the realm of fantasy. My answer was very clear: "Imagine a child who has a fantasy of being Superman and runs around the house playing Superman all day. That's all well and good, because he's enjoying his imagination. What would happen if that child were to jump out the window and try flying like Superman? What would happen to that child? You don't even want to imagine it, right?" I asked him a second time. "This experience that you've told me about may seem harmless, but people have many bizarre sexual fantasies. And some of these are as dangerous as flying out the window."

During the fantasy, your mind plays the roles that it wants to, and this is a very creative mental activity. Fantasies are valuable and necessary for human beings. We must never rid ourselves of them. We should definitely accept them and not judge them, but acting them out is something that we must seriously think about. In what way would any particular fantasy affect your life?

Common Male Fantasies

In the past it was assumed that men were more likely than women to have sexual fantasies and that they had more of these fantasies during the act of masturbation or coitus. But in reality, women have developed this erotic component to a very high degree, though only in recent centuries has it begun to be expressed openly.

A lot of women's fantasies also coincide with men's. The most frequently mentioned male sexual fantasies are the following:

- To have sex with several women at once.
- Sexual acts with other men. It is worthwhile to point out here that in both women and men, having sexual fantasies about

being with someone of the same sex does not necessarily mean that you are homosexual. It may be due to the fact that all of us, women and men, had physical contact with both our mother and our father from the time we are born. Many times both sexes feel attracted to women who are vital and strong and/or to men who appear more passive. Fantasies about same-sex encounters occur more frequently than people care to admit. There is so much negative judgment against these fantasies that some people feel guilty about having them and repress them completely. If this produces too much anxiety, you should definitely consult with a professional.

- Role-playing, such as doctor, teacher, bus driver, plumber, electrician or chauffeur.
- Group sex.
- To make love with singers, models, movie stars or others with power and fame. This fantasy is common in both men and women.
- Having sex at work, at school, with teachers, bosses or coworkers. This fantasy is also common in both men and women.
- Sadomasochistic fantasies in which violence has a special appeal. While mixing pain with pleasure, the man may play either submissive to or dominant over a woman who is either meek or authoritative.
- To ambush his wife from behind. For this fantasy, the best position is the surprise posture from the Kama Sutra. This posture is ideal for those who love savage, primitive-style sex. The man, standing, "surprises" her by penetrating from behind and marking the rhythm for coitus. She relaxes her entire body letting gravity pull her hands to the ground. For her, the stimulation is concentrated in the angle of the opening of the vagina, which provokes a sensation of tightness that is very pleasant for a lot of women. For him, the most powerful sensation expands from the glans as it penetrates the vaginal opening at will and stimulates the clitoris during its most daring thrusts. The man's visual field includes her anus, her buttocks and her back, areas which

are extremely erogenous for many men. The domination that he expresses coupled with her total relaxation benefit the man's ability to play with her anus. You can find more information about the positions described in the Kama Sutra, complete with illustrations, in my book *Sex and the Perfect Lover,* published by Atria Books.

Remember, erotic fantasies can be a wonderful enrichment to your sex life, but may become negative when they impede normal sexual functioning as in the case of a man who can't be aroused without watching pornographic videos.

Women's Sexual Fantasies

Many women share similar ideas when it comes to their most common fantasies.

- To be his queen: she needs to feel her man contemplating her and giving her his total attention. She likes to be kissed from her ankles to her back, awakening sensations that come from some other place beyond the vagina. This image, more than a mere fantasy, is a very common desire in most women.
- To take her clothes off and dance for him, to do a striptease. This erotic fantasy provides stimulation and predisposes women for pleasure when acted out with one's partner.
- To have sex in public or in front of video cameras.
- To have sex with a stranger and to never see him again. This desire is rooted in the fact that many women are tired of being ladies in bed, of making love surrounded by softness all the time. Some women would actually like their husbands to treat them more savagely. Perhaps an alternative to this fantasy is to have your partner act as if he has just met you, without any delicacy, roughly and having his way with you.
- Being taken and sexually dominated by one or more men.

- Lesbian sex with another woman.
- Having sex with ex-lovers, and allowing her current lover to watch.
- Exhibitionism: showing her body in public while everyone watches.
- Totally dominating a man. I recommend the amazon posture for this. Assuming a totally active position, the woman can be on top and control the rhythm of intercourse, straddling her partner with her feet planted firmly on either side of his body. This position is perfect for active women who are comfortable in a dominant role and like to control the pace of sex. For the man, this is an amazing experience, because it allows him to be passive and to relax during sex. The man can touch his lover's breasts, kiss her neck and caress her hair while she moves over him. This visual angle provides an exciting view for the man, allowing him to clearly see his lover's every movement. The woman will also derive much pleasure from knowing that she is in control and that her lover knows it.
- Wearing sexy or nearly nude clothing to a party and attracting the attention of all the men and women.

Sex play and fantasies may be awakened among men and women at any time, but it should always be a natural act. The couple should be able to share the workings of their respective imaginations with ease and freedom, without fear of criticism or judgment.

Experiences with Sexual Fantasies

Here are two examples of sexual fantasies submitted by readers:

Aura, age forty-two: *I am a composer and have played piano since I was a child. I always had fantasies of making love on top of my piano. I even imagined myself making love while performing a concert in public. I've also had fantasies about having sex with my husband on top of* the horse that we have out in the country and riding naked on the horse all over our ranch while the other women die of envy. I think it's a cute idea. I've told my husband about it and he laughs a lot but I'll never act it out. Besides, I think that the very essence of fantasy is freedom and you have to accept the fact that human sexuality has such a wide range of tonalities that can be explored in the imagination.

Carlos, age thirty-seven: *I love it when my wife dresses up like a schoolgirl or wears sexy lingerie before we make love. I've had a lot of fantasies about younger women and my wife and I decided to play this game, which stimulates me sexually and allows her to feel younger and more creative. To me, the worst thing that can happen to any relationship is to get stuck in a routine, because that leads to boredom. That's why everything that helps to ward off monotony is healthy, wholesome and good for the relationship.*

What Blocks Erotic Fantasies?

What keeps people from accepting their own fantasies? Basically, it's the fear of being discovered and considered extravagant, sick, perverted or oversexed. We spend so much time trying not to have fantasies that this often blocks our relationship with ourselves and with others.

People with high self-esteem accept their own worth and consider themselves to be deserving of love. They have an easier time accepting their own sexual fantasies. And acceptance of sexual fantasies—whether lighthearted or dark—may be encouraged by our ability to understand them. Follow the exercise below to understand the erotic fantasies of your inner psyche (the images, feelings and sensations that sexually stimulate you) to help unblock your sexuality.

Find a comfortable position and close your eyes. If you like, turn on some relaxing music.

Step One: Breathe deeply and let your body relax every time you exhale. Think about the different fantasies you've had—sexual, erotic or romantic. They may be fantasies that you use regularly during acts of sex or masturbation, when you make love or those that entertain you while you take a walk or sunbathe. Pay attention to your physical responses while you think about each one.

Step Two: Remember the fantasies that you've had during your childhood, adolescence and adulthood. Imagine telling your fantasies to a group of people. Who are they? What are their reactions? What are you holding back?

Step Three: Now imagine yourself telling your fantasy to your lover, to your parents, to a priest and to your boss. Fantasize about people who represent authority figures, people whom you respect or admire, and people who love you. Note how you feel in each case, how your body responds and what types of judgments you are passing.

Step Four: Open your eyes slowly and on a sheet of paper, write down a description of each fantasy, the emotional and physical response that accompanied each, and your judgment of it. Don't censor yourself. If you feel shame, write about your shame. Show compassion for yourself. Remember to breathe, listen and remain present at every moment in order to know what you're feeling.

The experiences that we have explored in this exercise create the necessary conditions for understanding ourselves. If you can do this exercise with your partner, you will liberate your relationship from the phantom of shame and wipe out any negative beliefs that block your erotic potential.

Remember that all of us have fantasies. The important thing is to always recognize them, even if they seem unsettling; they can shed light on some important life experiences.

CHAPTER 22

I Love You and I Want to Make Love with You All the Time

Discover the journey of sex and forget about the final destination. Enjoy the sexual trip because it is a celebration of happiness and the consummation of the relationship. Making love offers an opportunity to experience eternity as the only time that exists.

Changing the Routine

Making love is a beautiful journey of the soul. It is a process of taking small, consistent steps to nourish love to its full potential. The more we experience the different techniques of love, and the more we alter our sexual routine, the more we become conscious of the powerful magic of sex. Not surprisingly, the mind is enthusiastically open to these new experiences.

If you truly wish to maintain the appeal of your sex life and the desire just as ardent as the first time, you must acknowledge the importance of this aspect of your life. Incorporate the unexpected, that which attracts two strangers at the onset and later causes them to fall in love, so that eventually each knows what the other is thinking, doing or feeling. The small gifts and details that we inject into our relationships are what keeps romance and sexual attraction alive: the intimate weekend getaways, the romantic dinners and such.

Sex at Different Times

Sexual harmony is a vital element for human health and longevity. When a man and a woman are able to make love with the frequency that both of them desire, they will obtain a degree of happiness and harmony that will project success and love onto every aspect of their lives. When a couple enjoys good communication, and can talk about these subjects naturally, asking one another their needs and desires, they can learn how to please one another and make stimulating changes in their love life. For example, try having sex in the morning or in the afternoon. There are no rules governing sexual desire. The best thing is to have it naturally express itself, but since we often don't have time or space for intimacy, it's wise to take advantage of any opportunities that may arise during the day. Here are a few examples:

Sex in the Morning: Some people like to make love as soon as they wake up, because that's the time at which they have the most energy. This schedule offers the benefits of spontaneity, and the couple is not awake enough to hold back anything. The unconscious world moves naturally within. Sensuality acts of its own accord. This hour frees us and transforms us; we forget established or studied attitudes, we forget to think too much. This is also a time when sexual fantasies crop up very easily. The only negative thing about making love at this hour is that many people have to worry about getting up to go to work. They may become afraid of relaxing too much and falling asleep after making love. But it's a great time of day to make love and I recommend that you experience its benefits.

Sex after Lunch: Many of us feel heavy after eating lunch. If, however, our meal has been light or particularly stimulating, and there's time for making love, it's actually a perfect time of day, especially for couples who have children in school.

Sex in the Afternoon: If it's possible for you to escape from work, steal off to an intimate bath with your partner at some special location. This indulgence at this very relaxing time of day can help to unleash your desires and obliterate the stress of the daily grind. Enjoy mutual relaxation and don't talk about the problems of the day. Obviously, if you're going through a very heavy work period, it's best to wait until the weekend or the evening for this type of an encounter.

Sex in the Evening: Especially among partners who have been married for years, it's normal to wait until the children are asleep and take advantage of that special time. Sex at night allows more space for the imagination to run wild, and generally takes place in bed. Never watch TV before going to bed if you really want to make love. You run the risk of falling asleep in front of it, which is anything but motivating.

Sex in the Wee Hours: Sex between states of sleep and wakefulness represents the most prized gem for those connoisseurs of the unintelligible and enigmatic passions of sexual love. When a couple is just starting out and feeling flamboyant and idealistic, often one of the two will wake up aroused in the middle of the night and incite the other partner into sex. Unfortunately, with the passage of time, sex at this hour becomes an extinct species that no ecological refuge can ever hope to save. No matter how tired you are, try at least once a month to experience sex during these hours of passion and fantasy.

Experiences with Sex at Different Times

Namur, age forty-seven: *I really enjoy morning sex with my wife. After we make love, we prepare a succulent, delicious breakfast and sometimes we bring it back to bed with us so that we can get right into eating and then making love. I get very excited when I get up early and prepare a scented bath for both of us. I like to put flowers in the water, or rose petals, especially on Saturdays and Sundays when neither of us has to go to work. The morning is a very positive time, because the kids are asleep, there's no noise to bother us and I'm usually way too tired at night after work. We found our solution and it really works for us.*

Miriam, age twenty-nine: *I woke up that day feeling a strange excitement. I felt as though if I didn't make love, I would explode. I had never felt that way before. I didn't know whether to masturbate or wake my husband up. I decided to touch his penis subtly and started kissing his back. He started waking up little by little and I was afraid he'd be angry because he had to work the next morning. But the fact was that he loved the idea, so we started to rock gently together between the sheets without turning on the lights. We found a unique elasticity and a special kind of synchronicity that we had never experienced until then. After that very special sexual act, we decided to do it that way at least once a week. We find it lots of fun and very stimulating. A lot of times I've caught him mumbling in his sleep while we're making love. It's an experience everyone should have. I will always remember those nights with great pleasure.*

Different Places in Which to Make Love

In order to experiment with sex, you have to have a loving spirit and adopt a new attitude. The capacity for acceptance of the unexpected will make sex much easier and more fun. Some couples like or need to change their habits and find other places or other situations in which to have sex to keep their sex life from becoming monotonous.

If both parties are willing, it is easy to explore new territories. A new setting will recharge the experience, even if you are making love with a partner who you've been with one thousand times. Below are some different places where you can make love without having to spend lots of money. All you need is creativity and willingness.

Camping: Even if you live in a tiny apartment or in a house with several rooms and a garden, find a spot where you can set up a tent. On a special day, when you're certain that you're not expecting company, call your partner at work and tell him or her that you're going to camp out in the garden that evening, or at some other special location. Choose a refreshing beverage that you both like (alcoholic or not), prepare a light meal or pack some cold cuts with fruit, or some sandwiches, and put them into a basket as though you were really going camping. Don't forget to set the mood with candles, and find a way to play music that you both love. Spread a blanket on the ground, or an air mattress if you prefer. When your partner arrives home, everything should be set up so that he or she can walk directly into the environment that you've created without thinking about what happened at work or other problems.

I have played this little game with my husband. Actually, it was his idea and it really is a lot of fun. It brings you back to your childhood and adolescence, making intimacy more spontaneous and especially romantic because partners forget how old they are.

The Bath: The bath has never lost its effectiveness when it comes time to make love—it's a very intimate location. The steam rising from the water, the use of fragrant oils or aromatic salts—all of these things can offer an ideal state of relaxation for lovemaking and for taking all the time in the world to explore and play with each other's bodies. After taking a relaxing shower, run a luxurious bath and take special pleasure in making love in the water. If either of you are resistant to this method of lovemaking, make up some excuse to call your partner into the bathroom and ask him or her to rub a little cream on your back to relax you, or something along those lines. There are many products available that generate heat and excitement as soon as you rub them on your skin. Next, ask your partner to remove your clothes for you, then to take a bath with you. The rest depends on each of you and your fantasies.

Quickies and Forbidden Places: All of us have fantasies of making love in a strange place: a dark alley, a terrace, an elevator or on the stairway of the building in which your parents or in-laws live. Although it is dangerous, the taste of risk is highly exciting. Couples who live together often make sure to have sex that is slow and sensual, valuing what goes on not only during the act, but also before and after. But sometimes, when circumstances are appropriate, the urgency of desire or the thirst for an adventure may lead you to enjoy a "quickie," because you both simply cannot wait.

The sensation offered by a quickie is like the titillation of an unexpected seduction, the thrill of conquest. It is a challenge for both seasoned lovers and those who love to experiment. The positions used during quickies are often kinky and different from the norm. A lot of men and women experience more arousal when they feel their partners touching them through their clothing. This sensation can be doubly erotic. Others like to remember their teen years when they'd make love at their parents' house feeling that hot rush that intensifies the terror of being caught. Some enjoy sex in exotic locations such as an abandoned beach or in a secluded meadow, while others are excited by public restrooms or movie theaters. Still others dream of doing it on a train, an airplane or a boat. It's all a matter of preparing the set. Anything is possible with quickie sex.

Every Room in the House: It's important to abandon the bed and occasionally visit the dining room table, the kitchen counter and even the wet lawn in the yard. The main thing is to not get used to any one location because that would lead your libido down a dead end into routine, and nobody wants that. Before you have this experience, and to make it even more romantic, write a surprise note and leave it for your partner to find. Express how much you love and desire your partner, how much you love his or her touch, how much it excites you to make love when you're together. Talk about how your lover caresses your hair, stimulates your breasts, licks your genitals or covers you with kisses. This is a guaranteed trick to keep your partner excited and aroused all day after finding the note. He or she will chase you all around the house, wanting to make love in every room.

A Private Journey: How long has it been since the two of you took a few days off together with no distractions, no telephone, no kids and no interruptions? Plan a long weekend getaway to refresh your romantic relationship. Choose a secluded place, where nature will surround you with its magic and the two of you can feel free to enjoy yourselves away from your daily routine.

Relive the Very First Time: It is also interesting to go back and relive the erotic urgency and desire of your first few sexual encounters. Go back to the place where you made love for the first time or to the place where you first danced or dined together on that occasion. It's very sweet and romantic to remember these experiences every three months or so, if possible, or do it at least once a year, as it offers the couple a lot of strength and a sense of companionship and camaraderie. You might feel a little strange or out of place the first time you do it, but both of you will benefit greatly from the memory of those early encounters.

Work Abduction: Sometimes risk can be a sexual stimulant. If your lover works in an office and you know what time the other coworkers will be out, drop by with erotic toys, music, candles and maybe a cool beverage to break up the monotony of the tedious workday. Lock the doors and pretend that you are kidnapping your partner and will not allow any complaints. If you like, you can tie the person to a chair and arouse him or her by means of oral sex, massage and erotic touching. Celebrate sex and use total creativity with your partner, who may feel a little skeptical at first, but after the initial shock wears off, will be eternally grateful.

Sex Games

Erotic play allows lovers to try something new or something that they've been fantasizing about. Sex play allows you to dramatize an imagined situation, share it and express your needs to your partner. You can also liberate your mind this way and achieve a stronger union with your partner. Set up a good scene for erotic play; it should be adaptable to the bedroom and create a sensual and positive environment. I recommend burning incense and scented candles. Cover your lamps with sheer cloth to dim the lights; listen to soft romantic music; try to clean and tidy up the room. Once the environment is as romantic as possible, you will more easily be able to attract that very same energy to yourself. Here are some ideas for different sexual games that couples can play in their bed or anyplace where both of you are comfortable.

Perform in Public: This game allows for the marvelous possibility of liberating the exhibitionist in each of us. The idea is to pretend that you're on a stage and that there's an audience watching you while you have sex. You can record comments on cassette tapes and play them while you're making love. So for example, you might hear applause and someone saying "Bravo" while someone else makes the remark that "they are the best couple I've ever seen making love" or "they get so hot while they're having sex." Don't forget to throw in a few humorous things such as "oh, baby, you've got better legs than she does . . ."

Star in a Movie: Piggybacking on the previous game of "Perform in Public," the couple can videotape different segments of their lovemaking and later make a movie with it. It can be pornographic or artistic, depending on your imagination and taste. Later on, you can get all excited again while you're watching it. Another way to stir up excitement and sensuality is to look at yourselves in a mirror while making love. Watching yourself with your partner will allow you to experience new erotic sensations.

Submission: For many men, it is very exciting to let themselves be submissive and let the other person take control of them. The woman can act out the role of master while the man plays the role of the slave. The person who plays the master should be inflexible, creating an atmosphere of suspense, making it clear that she runs things and that the partner is defenseless against her authority.

Some tips for playing this game: Choose a "password" beforehand that means "stop now." It can be something simple, such as the name of a color. Cover your partner's eyes and tie his hands behind his back using a soft cord. Once you have him at your mercy, start provoking and arousing him. You may touch his erogenous zones using feathers or special textured gloves that you can use for different parts of the body. You can also use creams to stimulate his body. Later on, untie your slave and order him to take his clothes off slowly, constantly obeying your instructions. Surrender to the game, but be very careful to not do anything that might seriously injure or hurt the other person or both of you. The couple can also switch roles if they choose.

Costumes and Stories to Act Out

When the goal is raising the temperature in bed, why not get dressed up? You will undoubtedly leave your lover gaping in wonder. That's because creating situations and taking on characters is a game that could last all day and become the key to recovering the enthusiasm of your relationship.

Everything is permitted in the game of love. Wearing a costume for your partner is actually a lot more fun than you might think, because it enables you to transform a normal encounter into a session of unforgettable pleasure.

Costumes for Women: Wait until just before he comes home from work, when you know that you will not be interrupted by anyone, and dress up as a harem dancer. Find some appropriate music and rehearse a few steps. Take a few belly dance lessons before playing this game or watch an instructional video so that you can learn sexy and exciting techniques.

Some men love women who dress up as maids and wear aprons with sexy lingerie. Another costume that turns men on is the school-girl outfit, composed of knee socks and a short skirt under which you can see thighs and panties. The classic tight-fitting "Catwoman" leather suit is another favorite. Red devil costumes also turn men on; wear a sexy red top with tight pants. Or play a librarian, police officer or nurse to heat things up during erotic play. Try wearing a wig that is different from your natural hair to give yourself a totally different look.

Costumes for Men: These are somewhat less original and diverse, but they too have their charm if the wearer gets into the spirit of things and performs a sexy striptease. Possibilities include dressing up as a police officer, a firefighter or a soldier. These generally look very sensual. The man can also dress up as a gangster or gigolo, wearing a dark suit with a black shirt and white tie, or a white suit with a black shirt and white tie. He can pretend that his wife is a prostitute and force her to fulfill his desires. He can even pay her after sex if the couple wishes to take it that far. Once the woman catches on to this game, she should also dress provocatively for her role.

Another erotic game is for the man to dress up as some famous actor or singer whom his wife likes. It is fundamental to activate the imagination in both women and men in order to create interesting and entertaining stories. The idea is for the couple to pick roles and characters with which they feel comfortable. It's important to surprise women with these costumes, but men should remember that women are very intuitive and pay attention to details. That means the man must be careful to keep the surprise a secret.

This type of sex play adds an undeniable element of fun to the relationship and helps strengthen the bond between lovers.

Card Games or Chess

Erotic card games also allow or suggest things that a couple hasn't tried before, although nobody can force you to do anything that you don't want to do. There are lots of card games that can be played in bed such as poker, canasta, gin rummy and others. Some couples also play games like backgammon and chess, or anything else that they find fun and interesting. The idea is that whoever wins gets a prize: the winner can make the loser do anything he or she wants. Never suggest anything that the loser wouldn't be in agreement with. The winner gets to decide any of the following:

- The sexual position used and for how long
- The type of role play and sex game that will be played
- The type of caress wanted
- Whether to be sexually stimulated and on which area of the body
- Whether to add a sex toy to the game
- The location in the house for sex or the setting of the next sex date

TIPS FOR PLAYING EROTIC GAMES

- Concentrate on feelings of pleasure and how to share them.
- Cancel any negative associations that arise and don't think about rejection; if you're not ready to play at that moment, choose another occasion.
- Plan a day for erotic game-playing. Choose different locations, just as when you plan a party, but always make sure to do it with the desire to have fun.

- While you're experiencing a new game or location, relax and allow your imagination to soar. While listening to soft music, close your eyes and open your mind to erotic images. These provide a potent aphrodisiac.
- To play is to have fun, and only intimacy and trust will allow you to comfortably dress up and act out different characters to express your multitude of personalities.
- Playing in unfamiliar spaces allows you to totally focus on your partner, to laugh, share jokes and experience the freedom of visiting different places when you feel like making love—in every sense of the word.
- In order to play safe, you can set the scene in advance. If you know your role beforehand, you will feel more confident and secure. You could even write out some dialogue ahead of time, although there are those who prefer to use their imagination in the moment. With a little practice, you will feel more and more freedom to improvise every time you play.
- Always remember that you are playing a game. Under no circumstances should anyone ever feel manipulated or forced to do something he or she doesn't really want to do. You should ideally find a game, or series of games, that satisfies the fantasies of both partners.
- Depending on how much fun you want to have during sex, you can create a grandiose scene with costumes and locations, or you can play in the privacy of your own home. For this reason, accessories are sometimes useful, though what really matters is the fantasy that both of you are enjoying.

Experiences with Erotic Games

I received these two comments in response to my book *Sex and the Perfect Lover:*

Jim, age thirty-three: *It's hard to find new ways to add more fun and zest to sex. But then a voice activates itself, something happens and suddenly it's begun. One of you decides to make love inside the closet at a friend's house, or in a forest under the shade of a tree. I practiced a lot of these ideas with my wife before we got married, but later on we got into a rut and forgot these things. The other day I was reread-ing your book* Sex and the Perfect Lover, *which talks about different positions. We remembered how we used to make love in the car beside a lake, using a very unusual position because my car was tiny. So we headed off to the lake in the car, but we actually got up the nerve to get out of the car and do it. We had an inflatable mattress with us and a set of sheets, so we pretended we were camping. It was fun. We made love for an hour and a half and then got back in the car and continued playing. We came up with an idea to take a short vacation away from the kids. What I enjoyed most was not just the sexual act, but experiencing the beautiful smell of the forest and her skin and hair. We seemed to have that same vigor and excitement that we did when our relationship was just starting. We even found ourselves trembling at the same time from the pleasure and fear of being caught. It was a brilliant experience and I'd recommend it to any couple.*

Danielle, age twenty-nine: *In my five-year relationship, the way we play before having sex is to have fun doing things that make us feel like teenagers. That's our way of relaxing before making love after a hard day at work. There's nothing hotter or sexier to us than making one another laugh. The variations are endless: we tickle each other, then we wrestle without hurting each other, and of course to score a point one has to pin the other partner on his or her back on the bed. Then we get into having sex. We also do dirty dancing. We make up situations and improvise as though we were in a club. My husband pretends that he doesn't know me and asks me to dance. I pretend to turn him down and then we play and laugh until we can't help but feel totally happy and then we make love. Sometimes it seems like we're drunk on hap-*

piness. The good thing about pretending to meet each other in a club is that we start seducing each other and saying hot little things to each other like we did the first time we met. It's a way of remembering how much we really like one another. Also, we sometimes pretend to be doctor and patient, or teacher and student . . . it depends on what mood we're in that day.

Sex games grant a couple time and permission to get to know one another, to find each other effortlessly. That will yield plenty of pleasure for both of you and allow the relationship to last longer. Reviving desire and love is the responsibility of both partners in the relationship. Why not use all of these methods in order to have more fun, get to know each other better, develop mutual trust and "get your groove back"? In fact, you could even use these techniques after sex to get things going again.

Sex Toys

Just a few decades ago, nobody talked about sex toys. Today they are sold even as key chains, not to mention all of the other varieties. In reality, these colorful and popular toys have existed for over twenty-five hundred years. Ancient Egyptians and Greeks used dildos, as did the Romans, who also carved giant candles that resembled enormous penises.

Some of these toys were very imaginative. The Chinese "urchin" was a circle of fine feathers attached to a silver ring that was worn around the penis. There are still many Chinese manuscripts around today that explain how to tie the base of the penis with silk in order to maintain an erection (this is a primitive version of the modern "playboy ring").

Dildos: In their most basic form, dildos are essentially replicas of the male penis and are used as masturbatory aids. But as dildos have changed over the ages, so have their uses. Some new models are even double-headed, allowing couples to enjoy mutual penetration.

Vibrators: A lot of people consider a vibrator the best sex toy of all. Their size and shape can resemble dildos but, as their name implies, they run on battery power and vibrate. In fact, the latest models not only vibrate but also rotate and move, and many come with different attachments to provide a variety of sensations.

How do you choose a good vibrator? The number of vibrators on the market is really amazing. You can find them in different sizes, styles, materials and shapes, which may either inspire you or overwhelm you. There are a number of factors to consider that will make this task a bit simpler and definitely more pleasurable.

How do you plan to use it? Maybe you need a good multiple-use vibrator that can be used for insertion and clitoral stimulation at the same time. Or maybe you'd prefer a phallic-shaped vibrator that is designed for penetration but can be applied directly to the clitoris. If you like a little action in the shower, a waterproof vibrator is best for you. These stay cleaner because they come into contact with running water, and are easier to clean by virtue of being waterproof. Just remember that a waterproof vibrator is not as powerful as a dry one and when submerged, its vibration is less powerful than when it is dry.

The Jackrabbit or Playful Tongue: This is a fun toy that works like a vibrator but uses a "tongue" (shaped like rabbit ears) that works on battery power and vibrates to simulate oral sex when applied directly to the clitoris.

Chinese Ben-Wa Balls: Ben-Wa balls are small balls that are made of metal and usually covered with latex. They are about the size of golf balls, soft, with bumps along their surface and joined together by a cord. The balls are introduced into the vagina, where they move and provoke a sensation of sexual stimulation.

Ben-Wa balls were used by women in ancient China as therapy for improving their sexual relationships. Once introduced into the vagina, they dilate and prepare the vaginal walls for more pleasurable intercourse. You can insert the balls moments before having sex or you can walk around with them inside of you all day. The vibrations produced by the tiny balls enclosed inside each one increase the natural lubrication of the vaginal walls, which contributes to better sex. The modern motorized version of these balls serves to stimulate the deepest areas of the vagina and the G-spot.

Handcuffs: This is an essential must-have for lovers of sadomasochism or bondage. Handcuffs assure that only one partner has control over his or her hands during the exchange.

The Playboy Ring: Made of transparent silicone and with a vibrating element that attaches at the base of the penis, this ring serves to directly ignite feminine pleasure. Its function is simple: it has a small on/off switch and a battery life of approximately twenty minutes, which can be extended if you turn it off. It doesn't provide much stimulation for men, but it stimulates the clitoris at the moment of maximum penetration during intercourse.

Experiences with Sex Toys

Jackie, age forty: *For us, sex toys are therapeutic. You can find them anywhere in sex shops, but I always buy mine online. It's just easier and I feel safer that way. For the past five months my husband and I have been using these and it helps us to relax from the anxiety that he always feels when he's trying to get an erection because I want sex. This way, he plays with me using the toy, and after I have my orgasm, I play with him. You can only imagine the rest. I recommend buying those that come with instructions for use and help to work through any psychological issues the user may have.*

Sexual play and sex toys are options that enhance your enjoyment and also liberate you from external pressures. Playing these games before coitus is fundamentally important, but don't forget to also kiss and caress the whole body as a means to truly reach and connect with your lover's heart.

CHAPTER 23

I Love You and
I Love the Magic of Our Union

The magical sexual vibration is very attractive at the start of a relationship, but you need to enrich it daily and nourish it with sexy and affectionate ingredients in order to keep your relationship as special as it was initially. It is very important to know how our vital energy works as sexuality in order to fully enjoy every instant of our lives.

Erotic Energy and How It Works

Sex generates a very high chemical vibration through the body's five physical senses. During sex, the body is capable of channeling and expressing itself in a potent and powerful way. In order to enjoy your sexuality fully and intensely, it is important to learn how to physically feel that sexual vibration. If we don't know how to use that energy we will not be able to fully develop our senses and the sensory organs that are essential to our erotic enjoyment. We have learned to express our sexuality in a way that is focused exclusively on the quick and fleeting orgasm, as though the genitals were the only organs in our bodies. This is due to the deeply rooted repression that exists particularly in Western society.

We must learn to think of sex as something that naturally flows as anything else in our life. In reality, as the sexual beings that we are, sexual energy is vital and fundamental to our lives. If we experience sex as a part of the great spirit of creation, we can understand that the physical body, sexuality itself, the mind, feelings and organs are in no way separate from our spiritual beliefs and principles. With this in mind, we can enjoy our sexuality fully, on both the physical and the spiritual level.

Eastern mystics have left behind millenniums full of teachings about the power of sex and its magical energetic capacity. In recent times, scientists have actually discovered the same properties. Scientific studies affirm that sexual excitement and the act of sex produce truly profound chemical changes in our bodies, and that sex hormones are responsible for these changes. Hormones are chemical messengers secreted by endocrine glands into the bloodstream. They travel through the bloodstream and provoke all the phenomena associated with sexual response, from the gleam in your eye, to the dilation of your pupils, to the consistency of your erection. The word *hormone* is derived from the Greek word *hormano,* which means to wake or arouse.

This dance of hormonal energy affects the functioning of the entire body in a very positive way, increasing the production of sex hormones (estrogen in women and testosterone in men) and adrenaline, a hormone that predisposes the individual toward sex. When production of these hormones becomes stimulated, blood circulation improves, and the immune system is flooded with substances that help to strengthen it. Sexual arousal is also stimulated by substances known as endorphins that produce sensations of pleasure and satisfaction. The largest amount of this substance is released into the bloodstream during orgasm. At this moment all the nerve cells in the brain fire their electric and energetic charge, provoking absolute physical relaxation. The hormones released during sex also fight stress by relaxing all of the body's muscles, contribute to positive moods, and retard aging by improving circulation in the body. Later in this chapter we will discuss in more detail the functions of erotic energy and its benefits.

A couple that achieves a satisfying sex life functions better in all the other areas of their daily lives. Yet we must not think that sex itself magically solves everything. Working on the relationship, constant seduction, companionship, honesty and trust are also essential ingredients for enriching your erotic chemistry and supporting your general well-being.

Elements That Fire Up Sexual Energy

Human beings are pure energy and loving vibrations. Through sex, we can express the maximum level of these qualities to our loved ones, especially in the culminating moment of orgasm.

In the previous segment we explained the functions of erotic energy and its physical sensations. But the question arises: If these mechanisms that the body generates are so perfect, why don't we feel the same sexual vibration during all of our sexual experiences or with every single partner that we've ever had? The answer is physical, psychological and spiritual. From the very earliest point of attraction, seduction or commitment, to the sexual act itself with orgasm as its summit, everybody experiences different psychophysical conditions and states of spiritual consciousness. These are caused by the stimulation of certain nerve cells that trigger hormonal secretion and muscular contractions on the physical level. On the mental level, everything depends on our thoughts, on whether or not we think it's a positive thing to have sex on that day, at that time and with that person. If we're not into it mentally, the sex won't be very rewarding.

Our sexuality or feelings about sex may be very different depending on our emotional state and changes in our lives or our environment. In addition, we don't always feel the same intensity with the same person. This means that not everything depends on each partner's skill, knowledge or level of sexual experience. Our capacity to enjoy sex depends as well on the conscious willingness of the two partners, on the love exchanged between them and on all the other elements produced within a relationship that we have discussed throughout this book.

We must understand that we are born with all the infinite potential necessary to enjoy our bodies, to experience happiness, to feel ecstasy and to expand our erotic vibration to the maximum degree of magic, because our bodies were conceived this way by divine order. It is only our social conditioning and moral codes that may be blocking us.

In order to have a pleasing and powerful sex life, we must recognize our bodies as a source of total pleasure and creation. We must learn to feel and express all that lives inside our bodies and souls, to express our feelings and personalities. We must learn to manifest and develop with intelligence and freedom the capacity to love, for the purpose of creating and nurturing relationships that are truly and totally healthy. If we can make this emotional, physical, spiritual and mental resonance express itself, we will be able to enjoy life in a way that is completely holistic and limitless.

Experiences with Sexual Energy

Freddy, age thirty-four: *I feel such pleasure when I make love that I sometimes praise the erogenous zones, mine as well as my partner's. For example: "Your breasts are so beautiful today!" "The lips of your vagina are so pink that I love them!" and things like that. It's kind of a nice way to relish the pleasure that I get from sex. It's also a way to break from the routine and give the body a boost using positive energy.*

Melinda, age twenty-nine: *I learned the importance of using every part of my body. I always start every session with my partner with a nice relaxing massage. It leaves our skin feeling soft and alleviates the tension of the day. I focus on his back, shoulders, head, hands, feet. I eventually cover his whole body, and when we're really relaxed and sensitive, that's when we start playing with our erogenous zones. It's so nice to kiss his feet, and I love running my tongue up the inside of his legs, behind his knees, brushing by his face and barely touching it, the*

heat generated by our hands. After sex I feel healthier than ever. I feel
as though it expands all my energy as a human being.

How to Keep Erotic Energy Alive Forever

Here are a few facts to help you positively change the patterns of
your sexual vibrations and increase your erotic energy and its magic.
These are guidelines that we should remember and repeat to ourselves at those times when we feel guilty about enjoying our own
sexuality.

As explained in the first part of this book, you could even write
down in a notebook or personal diary the ones that vibrate most
harmoniously with your personal situation. The purpose of this
exercise is to modify any patterns blocking your sexual potential.

- Sex is fun, exciting, healthy and natural.
- Making love can burn up to 560 calories, and that is the equivalent of one and a half hours of riding a bicycle. The exercise and
  movements involved in the sexual act help tone all of the body's
  muscles.
- Sex is an instant cure for mild depression. It releases endorphins
  into the bloodstream, producing a pleasant sensation of euphoria and well-being. The sexually active body secretes a greater
  number of pheromones, which are substances that attract other
  people with similar intentions.
- Sex improves the overall performance of both the body and the
  mind.
- Sex is the world's best tranquilizer.
- When practiced with regularity, sex improves mental health; it
  brings emotions to the surface, especially laughter, which alleviates stress.
- Through sex, people experience sensations of having limitless
  horizons and boundless power, and they abandon notions of
  time and space; they feel ecstasy, amazement, devotion and

finally, the experience ends with the conviction that something extremely important and valuable has taken place. The person feels totally transformed in some way and is thus strengthened and fortified by the sexual experience.

- Those who practice sex with love experience profound feelings of identification, sympathy and affection for others, even when they were feeling anger, impatience or disgust before sex.
- Through sexuality, one can play, feel joy, dance and marvel at one's power of seduction.
- Sex helps ward off boredom, anguish, guilt, irritability, sexual repression and psychosomatic illnesses.
- Through sexual experience, we can feel ourselves navigating an ocean of delight, satisfaction and inner peace.
- The different sexual positions help to cure all types of ailments such as weakness in the bones and variations in blood pressure, circulatory problems and even menstrual irregularity in women.
- The contractions that take place during coitus and orgasm tone the pelvic muscles, thighs, buttocks, arms, neck, thorax and other areas. In fact, making love several times a week improves posture and strengthens the lower abdomen and buttocks in both men and women.
- If you suffer from insomnia, sex may help you to avoid taking drugs. The biochemical changes that take place during lovemaking provoke relaxation and drowsiness almost instantly.
- Sex reduces the risk of cancer and coronary illnesses, and even helps to keep us looking young longer.
- During orgasm, our body pumps oxygen into all of our organs, which improves the flow of essential nutrients to the skin.
- A satisfying sex life enhances overall self-esteem. Is there anything more beautiful to look at than the gleam of sexual satisfaction in a person's eyes?
- Do you need to speak in public? Take advantage of the calming power of sex. The increase of hormonal levels during orgasm produces relaxation, mental clarity and releases inhibitions.

NURTURING LASTING PASSION

Sometimes it's not easy to keep passion and desire alive, but you can learn to do this as you get to know each other and your relationship matures. Here are some tips that synthesize many of the points that have been made in this book.

- The secret lies in treating sex ceremoniously. Prepare all the steps in detail; take your time to become internally ready for that moment of sexual exchange, which should be treated as a moment of major significance in the life of each partner.
- Try to stay alert to the look and mental state of your partner. Find opportune moments (these can be anytime, anywhere) when you can say something to each other while winking an eye. In particular, use code words that hold a special meaning for both of you. Try to tempt your partner into making love somewhere "forbidden" or wherever you feel lots of excitement.
- Celebrate events intimately. Evoke moments during which you felt that special chemistry and drink to them. Set out flowers, aromatic oils and candles to create a romantic climate that will elevate your excitement to its maximum level.
- Watch yourself make love. Do you do it mechanically like someone completing a business transaction, or do you need to surrender to passion more? Pay attention to your partner's reactions, looks, gestures. Caress your lover's entire body and express plenty of erotic intensity with every movement.
- Do whatever your partner loves. Always check to make sure you are doing everything that he or she desires and if not, try to do so. This could include whispering erotic stories in your partner's ear, or dressing up in some kinky and special way.
- Stimulate and provoke your partner sexually. Then, pull away and do something else until your partner chases after you with passion.
- Positive sexual fantasies serve to intensify your arousal, but it's

best not to remain attached to the mental image and to surrender instead to the physical experience.

- Tense the muscles of your buttocks in order to intensify your sensations and when your body is about to reach an orgasm. Express your erotic sentiments without censorship. Surrender your entire body to the pleasure.

- The main thing is that when you are making love with your partner, don't forget to communicate with gestures that are affectionate and say "I love you." This constant affirmation is an indispensable step in maintaining the balance of chemistry in love.

Sexual energy offers support and stimulation for the couple's relaxation and for each partner individually. It also allows the couple to experience a strong degree of unity and inner fusion. This is reflected in every area of our life.

CHAPTER 24

I Love You from the Center of My Being

Sex in its most elevated expression is divine, because only creation could have produced such an immense force that can manifest life and transport us in a single instant to such a special and beautiful paradise that we can reach out and touch the sky.

Sex Nourishes the Spirit

During the sexual act, the couple is fused, one into the other, physically in a way that is impossible to achieve on any other level or through any other form of contact. This fusion is not limited to the physical plane, because the emotional, mental and spiritual levels are also playing a role in the experience. This instant is so magnificent that everything in it is perfect. During that moment of orgasmic ecstasy, opposing forces come together in such harmony that they constitute the best possible nourishment for the spirit.

Awareness of the spiritual realm is essential to understanding one's relationship with oneself and with the entire inner and outer universe. Of course the spirit creates, transcends and expands the boundaries of your body. If you feel love toward your partner and there is a strong love connection between you, sex becomes a means through which to express your happiness and total fulfillment.

Sex can produce states of total illumination, increased inner sensitivity, and ecstasy. In ancient China and other Eastern cultures, sex was considered so sacred that there were temples decorated with pillows, colors and rugs to enhance the setting for the consummation of love. As part of this love ritual, it was customary to sprinkle fragrant flower petals around the bedroom to create the best atmosphere for eroticism. The ritual also included using fruits, honey, chocolate, celery, nuts, almonds, figs, grapes, pomegranates, cherries and berries to feed one another. These ingredients were essential to "feasting" on one another's bodies. It is noteworthy to point out that in many modern Western societies, this method of preparing for sacred sex or love magic has also been adopted.

Stimulate all of the senses freely by wearing attractive and sensuous clothing, expressing freedom of movement and by using aromas and flavors that help to awaken and deepen the sexual appetite. Ancient Chinese philosophy was based on the idea that the couple would meet in this unique location that was designed specifically for the sexual act. But mystics also pointed out that it was necessary for the couple to "build their own temple" before making love. When they refer to "their own temple" they don't mean a concrete external place. Rather, our bodies are sacred and so is sex. For this reason, we should adopt a sort of cult under which we worship our relationship as one would when attending a temple, church or any other place of religious worship.

As in every ritual, the erotic act includes factors that are very important for "Eastern"-style sex. One of these is breathing softly through the nose, relaxing the body, forgetting all else—including what's going on all around you and what might have happened today. The only thing of any importance should be the pleasure of enjoying the present moment.

The other necessary requirement is to free one's own body, appreciating it and inciting one another mutually to express the best qualities in each, free of embarrassment. A lot of these techniques have been explored and elaborated on throughout this book, not only as far as sexual contact goes, but also in order to reach a greater level of intimacy and understanding with both yourself and your partner.

As part of the erotic ritual, Asians recommend that upon completing the sexual act, the couple should not move physically far from each other, as that is an extremely sensitive moment in which it is beneficial to remain together, sharing tenderness and all the positive experiences that both have just enjoyed.

Ceremonial Sex

The idea behind this ritual is to treat sex as a celebration or feast. You should both prepare by wearing especially sensuous clothing. Also take time to mentally prepare yourselves to experience this as a significant moment in your relationship.

Ceremonial sex does not necessarily require a special location; you can do it at home, though it might be nice to set a special date for it. This ceremony has a rejuvenating effect on the couple, and the experience of doing it as a true ritual of love may completely transform your lovemaking experience. Here are some ideas for how to create the perfect setting for ceremonial sex. Add your own ideas to personalize your experience:

- Play stimulating or relaxing music, depending on your taste.
- Sing and/or dance together, or compose a chant or song.
- Enjoy a meal with plenty of aphrodisiacs.

APHRODISIACS

An aphrodisiac is any substance that enhances or increases the sexual appetite. The word is derived from the name of the ancient Greek goddess of love, Aphrodite. Some aphrodisiacs work by stimulating certain senses, such as sight, touch, smell or hearing, while others are ingested as foods or beverages.

Foods with aphrodisiac qualities include dried fruit, cinnamon, celery, chocolate, apples, pineapples, bananas, grapes, champagne, honey, fish, shellfish and sparkling wine.

Try this natural aphrodisiac for men and women:

Sex Truffles

INGREDIENTS:
3 dozen dates, pitted and chopped
6 teaspoons heavy cream
2 teaspoons rosewater or orange flower water
2 teaspoons chopped pistachios
2 teaspoons chopped walnuts
2 teaspoons chopped pine nuts
1 teaspoon grated fresh ginger
A few drops of vanilla
1 tablespoon toasted sesame seeds

PREPARATION:
With a mortar and pestle or food processor, mash the dates into a paste, then add the cream and rosewater, mixing thoroughly. Gently fold in the remaining ingredients, excluding the sesame seeds. Roll the mixture in your hands and shape into balls the size of marbles. Roll each small ball in the sesame seeds until it is fully covered. Place the small balls in a bowl, cover and chill. Each of you should consume three of the little balls during the sexual ceremony.

• Spend time feeding one another and licking wine off of one another's bodies. Kiss and caress your lover's body with genuine and pure passion.
• Share a shower or bath surrounded by exotic fragrances.

- Meditate using the techniques explained in this book before beginning any sexual contact.
- Massage one another to stimulate the erogenous zones.
- Learn the art of Kama Sutra, and experiment with different sexual positions.

If you follow all of this advice, you will not only be cultivating a much more lasting relationship, you will also enjoy making love as you've never enjoyed it before.

The secret to making ceremonial sex truly sacred is to enter into it as an elevated spiritual act and experience it as something out of the ordinary.

Experiences with Lasting Love

Lisette, age forty-six: *I've been with my husband for almost twenty-four years. I didn't have much sexual experience before meeting him, and I'm even sometimes ashamed to admit this, but the truth is that I love to enjoy sex with my husband. We've been through our crises, affairs, feeling wanton desire, but we always come back to one another because we can't help it. The most important thing we've found is a level of sexual maturity so great that even when we hold hands we do it with such pleasure that we don't even need to make love. We're drawn together by a feeling that is so special and spiritual that we can experience it with joy and celebrate every one of our encounters, as though it were our first time together. There's nothing more perfect than finding a lover with whom we can share commitment, friendship, companionship, sex and trust.*

Sexual Wisdom

One thing that strengthens relationships and makes for a dynamic sex life is the commitment and responsibility that each partner assumes in treating the other partner's pleasure as though it were his or her own. When two people are totally committed to one another, their relationship becomes deeper and more mature. Such a union creates the most fertile ground for truly powerful sex.

Below are some characteristics that determine whether or not you are prepared to experience spiritual sex in the context of a mature erotic relationship with your partner:

- Each of you understands, knows, processes and accepts the mental, physical, ethical, spiritual and social aspects of human sexuality.
- You are both open to learning and expanding all aspects of sex within the context of your relationship. You use visualization techniques and meditation to develop your inner wisdom and knowledge.
- You each maintain your sexual behavior within a set of carefully selected personal values that are constantly being reviewed and analyzed. These values are shared by each of you.
- You are each capable of discussing sex openly, and especially your sexual desires, blocks, problems or resistance to sex, physical contact or lack of sensitivity to your partner.
- Neither of you use seduction or sexual need to manipulate, harm or pressure one another.
- As mature individuals, you know and accept all aspects, limits, possibilities, enjoyment, responsibilities and consequences of your sexual activities.
- You each take an active responsibility in family planning and reproductive health.
- You know how to balance sexual gratification with other pleasures within the relationship and the family.
- You both enjoy a healthy diet and get plenty of physical exercise to assure better performance in the bedroom.
- You nurture communication and nourish it in open and sincere ways.

THE SEVEN ESSENTIAL PRINCIPLES FOR HAPPINESS IN LOVE

Affirm the following principles every day upon waking and just before going to sleep and, if you can, write them down in your date book or leave them posted where you can see them regularly. These principles are the basis for love within a successful relationship with yourself and with others. Recite these affirmations like a chant, repeating each sentence three times, at least twice a day.

1. My universe expands with unconditional love right here and now.
2. I am a paradise of love, here and now.
3. I am the creator of my experience of love and happiness every day.
4. My mind and my heart are pure and clean, beyond any external circumstances.
5. I am grateful for everything that happens to me, here and now.
6. Everything that I desire with love, I will do throughout this day for my own satisfaction and as an offering of joy to the entire universe.
7. Every being who inhabits the universe is my friend: I love them and they return the love to me.

True sexual liberation is spiritual and consists of a deep understanding that the human being is an entity composed of body, mind and spirit, and that these cannot act independently from each other. Sexual union is the means by which two whole and complete beings can merge their energies into one.

In my other books, you may find other points of view regarding spirituality, love and sexuality. My intention is to encourage you to journey through love knowing that each moment is the final destination. The only time and space that is important when you're in love is the eternal present. Because I now understand this reality at every level of my present life, I can say with total certainty: "I love you."

I Love You and I Want to Love You for the Rest of My Life

Love is a unique and fascinating experience that we must learn to keep alive through concrete acts. A relationship must be nourished and cared for. Relationships, like people, change as the years pass. Adjustments have to be made every now and then.

It's important to distinguish between the actual relationship and the conflicts and challenges that may arise within it. Conflicts should never be extended into other areas of the relationship, nor should they be used as an excuse to damage the relationship. For example, if you have a conflict around money, there's no need to extend it into the sexual arena. Many people use sex as a way to manipulate their partners. In a couple, all problems should be confronted with a positive spirit and the partners should work together to find solutions.

In this chapter, I synthesize the most important themes developed throughout the book based on my personal and professional experiences in keeping a relationship happy for life. The following points are offered for every couple to keep in mind and to apply every day.

253

Make It Your Top Priority to
Totally Commit Yourself to Your Partner

Most happy couples have built their relationship on solid and lasting foundations. Your relationship with your partner should be the most important commitment in your life. Think about what your partner genuinely needs, expects and wants from you. Without placing less value on your own needs, show appreciation for your partner's goals and achievements. Let your partner know that you will always be there for him or her. Demonstrate by your acts that in spite of the daily grind, your partner is always your number-one priority.

Your individual needs have to do with desires and aspirations that should be shared, discussed and fulfilled within the context of the relationship. Though you may have separate interests—one of you likes to paint, for example—each partner should support the other emotionally in these activities, even if he or she isn't personally interested in doing the same thing. This will make the other partner feel more confident and supported in whatever he or she chooses to do. If each partner pays attention to the other's needs, the couple will not fall apart in spite of difficult circumstances or periods of ups and downs. If you nurture your relationship daily through compassion, trust and love, nothing in life can ever come between you.

Spend Time Together
Enjoying Different Activities

Propose new and different activities to your partner, such as learning a language together or cooking for friends. These activities inject new life into the relationship.

Try to go out more often. Fresh air always renews love. Go out dining or dancing once in a while. You have no idea how much fun you can have by simply liberating your relationship from the four walls that enclose it.

Protect Your Partner's Health

A lifestyle that includes a healthy diet and plenty of exercise is always good for the couple. Massages, lotions and TLC also go a long way. Start each new year with a resolution to make your relationship healthier. Visit a gym together, or take up tennis, walking, jogging, yoga or some other physical activity.

Save Money for a Joint Project

The notion of saving money as a couple should not be limited to just saving for your wedding. You can save for a special vacation, a class, a summer home, a big party or any other project that you want to enjoy together.

Express Your Love
Frequently and Creatively

There are many ways to let your partner know how much he or she means to you. "Hi, darling; this note is just to let you know how much I love you." You can hide a little note like this inside a suitcase, purse or pocket. You can write the note on a sticky note, a card, a gift, a photograph or even the wrapper of his or her favorite candy. Think about a new way to surprise your lover today and let him or her know that he or she is the most important person in your life.

Don't Be Selfish

Selfishness has no place in a relationship. The best relationships are those based on the principle of giving in order to receive. If one of the two constantly practices this principle, it is highly probable that the other partner will reciprocate and offer the same level of spontaneous love, affection, dedication and consideration. Generous spontaneity is essential to true love.

Plan a Trip

Traveling together is one of the greatest experiences that a couple can share. Set some money aside weekly so that you can plan a special getaway with your beloved at least once every three months. You don't really need a lot of money for this; research some locations close to you that would be ideal for a weekend of rest and relaxation.

Avoid the Usual Preoccupations

What are the usual preoccupations in your life? Your job, the house, the kids, the laundry and so on; every one of us is plagued by a different obsession. Don't mention it; don't talk about it; don't let it disturb you. It will only cease to be a problem when you refuse to give it significance in your life. If it's a matter of making decisions, make them and accept the consequences.

We allow other people to hurt us by reliving painful experiences. Don't put all your time or energy into going over these matters again and again in your mind. Remember that as long as you are fine, everything around you will be fine as well. It's easier to think clearly when we take some space from our problems. By stepping back and shifting our attention to something else, we are able to come back to our original problem and see it in a new light.

Work with Your Partner on a Spiritual Level

Surround the relationship with a positive vibration. You have to think concretely and truly feel that which you desire in order to move your will toward the achievement of a particular goal. Feelings are an important engine in this process. Sit down with your partner at least once a week and establish positive affirmations to help you define and achieve your relationship goals. I do this spiritual work with my husband; we get together and come up with lists of things we want to achieve. We divide the list into two separate areas: our individual goals and the goals of our relationship. Then we discuss and explore all the ways to get our desired results.

Be Generous with Compliments

Paying a sincere compliment is a very simple way to soften your lover's heart. At least once a day, find something positive to say to your partner, as you did in the beginning of your relationship. Observe the points that make him or her special and praise these characteristics. People often remain silent when it comes to their admiration for someone, especially when that someone is their spouse. They may secretly admire the person but fail to mention these feelings of admiration to them. To reaffirm the joy in the relationship, you will need at least five positive comments to keep the love fresh and exciting. Smile, use all forms of flattery and every expression of fondness to nurture your partner. Go ahead and praise him or her right now.

Learn to Be Friends

Friends are there for us through thick and thin. They support us during our happiest moments and even more so during our most challenging difficulties. But they also speak their minds with no inhibitions because they totally trust their own criteria and have no need to pretend to be what they are not. And that is precisely what should happen in a couple: the two of you should be yourselves at all times and accept one another that way. Stay open to hearing your partner's comments without misinterpretations or taking things the wrong way. Above all, speak openly and frankly with one another.

Renew Your Trust

Today's couples must build their relationships on freedom and personal growth. If you respect your partner's personal freedom, you will have expanded the horizon for both of you within the relationship. Stop believing that if your partner wants time alone it means that he or she doesn't love you or that something has gone wrong in your relationship. We all need time alone. All of us are subject to having a bad day, and we all feel a bit strange at times. Learn to live with this and renew your trust in your beloved.

Accept One Another Mutually

Truly fortunate couples understand that loving means accepting the flaws in the other person. They know that an individual's desire to change emerges from the awareness of being accepted as he or she is. Far too often, we believe that love authorizes us to modify our partner's behavior and ways. We try to wipe out all traces of any unpleasant characteristics in our partner. Sometimes in this process, we actually downplay the same qualities that attracted us to him or her in the first place.

Nurture Intimacy in the Relationship

It's important to get to know your partner, to make love and to feel a genuine desire to spend time with him or her, sharing thoughts, existing in silence, learning how to live together; in other words, becoming sensitive to one another. Intimacy is not achieved through extraordinary events and exciting adventures scattered through time—though these may serve to nurture the relationship. Intimacy is the product of a multitude of shared experiences.

Be Open to Changes in Your Partner

Many of us think that a solid relationship is not altered from one year to the next. In reality, relationships inevitably change as people do. Couples who maintain a lasting relationship are flexible enough to accept change with a positive attitude.

Know How to Forgive

Forgiveness is an authentic and voluntary abandonment of anger and resentment. It is necessary in order for any good interpersonal relationship to flourish again after a crisis. On occasion, all couples hurt and disappoint one another. Then, one of two things occurs: either we forgive, or inevitably, little by little, we build up resentment. In order for love to endure, we must be capable of forgiving. To simply repress our feelings and emotions, or to ignore them, is not forgiving; nor is excusing the other person's behavior. It often happens that when we get into arguments, however insignificant, issues from the past come up and get used—even if they have little or nothing to do with the argument. Try not to bring up problems from the past. When you analyze what you're doing, you'll realize that you're only hurting yourself and damaging your relationship with haunting doubts that you have created. Behave like mature adults and practice forgiveness.

Seek Out Moments for Romance

Far too often, a relationship is weakened by lack of care. One of the foundations that keeps a couple together is the fire of erotic love. Emotional and sexual needs are fundamental in every individual. The sharing of mutual affection and delight that lovers experience together nourishes us each as people and reinforces our union. In order to achieve this end, consider the following suggestions:

- Say "I love you" at the most unexpected moments.
- Your opinions, differences or anything that separates you should never be allowed to enter the bedroom.
- Leave all problems outside of the bed and use sex to reinforce peace between you.
- Play special erotic games from time to time.

Celebrate with Your Partner

It's always good to celebrate and throw a party to mark special occasions. Don't think of holidays as merely a day off from work or school. It's important for the couple to create their own personal holidays, such as an anniversary or just a day to celebrate something special. Parties and celebrations have always helped recover the splendor of relationships and break up the daily routine.

Practice Greater Trust and Openness

All of us need to be able to share a secret, make a confession or trust someone with absolute credibility and with whom intimacy is guaranteed. To know that we can share our innermost secrets in full confidence is one of the most valuable aspects of intimacy. If every human being has secrets, so does every couple. The trust that intimacy implies prepares fertile ground for the act of opening yourself up without fear of betrayal, rejection or manipulation.

Choose Happiness

Human beings often attempt to compensate for their flaws, lack of self-love or insecurity through relationships. That is where they make their mistake. Happiness is rooted inside of our own being, but one has to be daring enough to savor it, to feel it. Happiness doesn't just happen to us; it is something that we ourselves accept without concern for what may be happening in spite of it. It is a choice, a personal attitude based on self-love that frees us from our addictions to pain.

Granted, happiness is not always easy to achieve, given the emotional and psychological blocks in our energy that cause us to repeatedly play out certain patterns that plunge our self-esteem to its lowest point. Nonetheless, this undertaking is worth all the effort it takes.

Here are some ideas that have been very useful for me and for people I have worked with. Buy a notebook in which you will plan your life. Draw a big smile on the cover or get some stickers with words such as *happiness, smile, joy, love, peace, wisdom,* or *power.* On the first page, write a list of questions regarding the things, feelings, thoughts or goals that you would like to accomplish. Don't write down any justifications about why you haven't accomplished them. The steps listed below will also help you to successfully improve your self-image and create more happiness in your life.

Step One: Dedicate the first page of this journal to appreciating yourself and to thanking the people who can assist you in accomplishing your personal goals. True happiness is about conquering challenges through effort. First, understand your true nature so that you can succeed at every level in life, especially in the area of love. Meditate deeply and serenely. Realize that in order to obtain what you want in life, you must recognize and accept how you really are above all else. Approve whatever it is you desire; this is an obligation you have to yourself. Give yourself the blessing to experience true happiness.

Step Two: Think of all of the things you do to make yourself happy and list them in a column. Note your thoughts, and try to fill your mind with positive and comforting ideas. Ask yourself what you want from life, then write it down.

Concentrate on every one of your goals, from the most important to the least. Above all, be attentive to thoughts that reveal how you perceive yourself. These thoughts shape your identity and the role that you play in your relationship, family, job or general environment. Every positive thought that you have will guide you one step closer toward success.

Step Three: In another column, list all of those things you do, either intentionally or unconsciously, that sabotage your happiness. Make notes regarding your emotional life. If you have negative thoughts and feelings, list those. Search inside yourself and identify your mistakes. Try to discover what thoughts, emotions and patterns are blocking you from being happy and which ones are contributing to your happiness. Identify in each list the mechanisms that interfere with or further each goal, so that you can modify those attitudes that keep you from finding happiness.

If you want to have a good relationship with someone else, you must cultivate self-esteem and value yourself first. Take time, even if it's half an hour a day, to review your goals and objectives and visualize them. Make it a point to learn the following:

- To think, rather than to react, during intense moments
- To assume the responsibility that you and your partner each have in damaging or nurturing the relationship
- To generate new options for your own behavior when old behaviorial patterns are no longer working for you

Once you have identified some solutions for improving your thought patterns, continue working in your journal on the following subjects.

Prepare a Timeline: Allow yourself a reasonable amount of time in which to accomplish a goal and write down the target date. Give yourself weeks, months or years depending on what the goal is. Setting a target date gives you an incentive toward continuing. Be considerate with yourself; it is better to establish a somewhat flexible timetable than a very rigid one. Remember that some things in life take more time than others, so don't be discouraged if your goal takes longer than you allotted. Plan to accomplish the goal on time, but be prepared to adjust the timetable if necessary. And don't pressure yourself to accomplish all your goals at once.

Keep Your Eyes on the Prize: Enumerate the rewards that you will enjoy once you've accomplished your goal. Before you begin, take some time to reflect on your principal goals and identify which of these are most important. Identify the reward that you will receive for accomplishing each of them. If your goal is, for example, helping others financially, think of the personal satisfaction that you will obtain from this act. Enumerate all of the benefits you will gain that will assist you in maintaining a high level of self-esteem at all times.

You will have to be genuinely convinced of your desires and their benefits; otherwise your intentions may not be powerful enough to mobilize the processes that lead to their manifestation. When you make your list of intentions, begin each declaration with the words "I WANT" in capital letters. Here are some possible examples:

"I WANT to be more conscious of negative messages that I think and the positive messages that I will replace them with."

"I WANT to take care of my body, by preparing healthy and nutritious foods and exercising at least three times a week."

Be sure to choose realistic goals that easily measure your inner emotional activity, and not goals that are vague or far off in the future, such as, "I WANT to be a human being who is loved by all."

Reflect on All Aspects of Your Life: Think about your relationship with your mind, body, feelings and spirit; with your job, lover, friends, free time or your home—it all depends on how you define your principal goals.

Periodically, you may need to add something to your list, or check off the goals that have already manifested in your life. You may also wish to review them or repeat them to yourself every day to reinforce your commitment to them. Ask yourself the following questions before writing down your new goals:

- What do I need to communicate to others about myself right now?
- What do I need to learn about myself in order to better myself every day?
- What do I need to reflect upon regarding each aspect of my experience?
- How might I be able to satisfy my need for change?
- How might I be able to establish more loving relationships?
- What values do I need to make concrete?
- How might I satisfy my need for beauty, peace or aesthetic experience?
- What new beginnings do I want to activate right now?
- What desires am I aiming to fulfill?
- How do I need to affirm myself?

The more clearly you can respond to your own questions, the more benefit you will feel, and over time you will become more and more efficient at translating your words, feelings and actions. Remember that every affirmation and answer to your questions must begin with the phrase *I want* and end with the phrase *here and now*. Both of these expressions are like magical energetic keys to your inner consciousness. They modify your subjective reality, and therefore, your life.

CULTIVATING HAPPINESS

Here are some rules to keep in mind for the purpose of helping you grow as a whole human being and achieving greater fulfillment:

- Live in the present; don't waste your life dwelling on the past or having anxiety about the future.
- Relax more, sleep better and be more focused.
- Accept the manifestation of emotions as part of human nature. Embrace and welcome your emotions.
- Learn to recognize your pent-up feelings and plan their liberation.
- Maintain a healthy diet and exercise routine.
- Resolve inner conflicts. The progress depends on you. Turn the pages of the past and revise, step by step, your life story. Observe your inner dialogue, recognize the positive aspects of your past and move forward.
- Feel vigorous and in control of situations; don't let anything surprise you.
- Respect others' opinions and elicit respect for your own.
- Do not try to control others' lives; direct that energy toward improving yourself instead.
- Wake up to fragrances, flavors, love, beauty, colors, music, people, fun, excitement, nature and happiness; eliminate fear, sadness, lack of trust and anger from your life.

This exercise may also be done using drawings that illustrate your feelings or thoughts. Another idea is to cut pictures from magazines that relate to each element you want to express. Remember that your mind and heart are responding to you, and this exercise will help you find the truth that is hidden there.

Perform the exercise serenely; choose the moment you like best

Mabel Iam

for working with yourself. Remember that everything you need is inside of you and that you have been blessed with the intelligence and ability to succeed in a relationship, as well as in work, school or anything else you wish to pursue in life.

The strategies and techniques suggested throughout this book will help you to control your inner reality, modify your emotional patterns and create a lasting relationship with the freedom and passion to constantly evolve together. Think of it this way: each of us is like a sailor who changes the angle of the sails on this boat that we call love according to our changing needs. When you are centered and happy, at peace with yourself and with each other, the unpredictable waves of time cannot forestall the amazing journey shared by you and your partner.

Epilogue

❧

I love to end my books with a message, with the aspiration and the hope that it will caress your soul, my beloved reader and friend. While writing to you, I feel a profound desire to travel through your eyes and to bless every single ray of light that has helped direct the focus of your vision on these letters—my thoughts that are now yours in words.

I Love

If I could see through the eye of my heart
I would notice that you are a part of me
That there are no differences between your masculine and my
    feminine
That your eyes reflect the stars in my own universe
That there is no need for you to penetrate my body
For me to feel you inside me, pumping like my own blood.

If I could perceive with the heart's eye each day
I would absorb every one of your vibrations
Without resistance, argument or hesitation
I would explore your naked soul before me,
Vulnerable and tender with limitless compassion.

*   *   *

If I could contemplate things with the heart's eye
Every place would be our home,
All of time would be infinite.

Now that I see with my heart
I affirm with a quiet scream "I love you"
Now and forever without doubt
Because I understand, from the eternal depths
Of my inner world
That we were never "two."

Now I can distinguish clearly that we are "one"
And this confirmation is not based on rational mathematics
But on the essential nature that transcends logic
Just as the sea and sand cannot exist without each other,
Nor the rainbow without the sun,
The sky without the horizon,
A kiss without the warmth of lips,
Or passion without desire,
You and I are one in the verb love
Conjugated in one tense, the now . . .
I Love.

Bibliography

Aristotle. *The Ethics of Aristotle: The Nicomachean Ethics.* Bookseller: Sumas, Wash., 1982.

Fisher, Helen. *The Anatomy of Love.* New York: Random House, 1994.

Gendlin, E. T. *Focusing.* Bilbao: Mensajero, 1983.

Horowitz, M. J. *Image Techniques in Psychotherapy.* New York: Behavioral Sciences Tape Library, 1974.

Iam, Mabel. *The Love Diet: Expert Techniques for Sensual Pleasure and Mind-blowing Sex.* New York: HarperCollins, 2006.

———. *Sex and the Perfect Lover: Tao, Tantra, and the Kama Sutra.* New York: Atria, 2005.

———. *El amante perfecto.* New York: Atria, 2005.

———. *Sex and the Erotic Lover.* St. Paul, Minn.: Editorial Llewellyn, 2005.

———. *El juego del amor.* St. Paul, Minn.: Editorial Llewellyn, 2005.

———. *Ser angelical.* St. Paul, Minn.: Editorial Llewellyn, 2005.

———. *El sueño del amor.* St. Paul, Minn.: Editorial Llewellyn, 2004.

———. *Qué hay detrás de tu nombre.* St. Paul, Minn.: Editorial Llewellyn, 2002.

———. *El don de la diosa.* Buenos Aires: Editorial Mega Libros, 2000.

———. *Escrito para vivir.* Buenos Aires: Corpo Solar, 1997.

———. *Tocando el cielo con las manos.* Buenos Aires: Editorial Latinoamericana, 1999.

———. *Tus protectores y guardianes de cada día.* Buenos Aires: Editorial Latinoamericana, 1999, 2000.

———. *Mano a mano con tu sabio interior.* Buenos Aires: Editorial Latinoamericana, 1999.

———. *Sanación con tus ángeles.* Buenos Aires: Editorial Vinciguerra, 1995.

————. *Guía con los ángeles.* Buenos Aires: Corpo Solar, 2001.

————. *Manual de conquista.* Buenos Aires: Corpo Solar, 2001.

————. *Tao del sexo y el amor.* Buenos Aires: Editorial Planeta, 2000.

————. *Diccionario de nombres con sus ángeles.* Buenos Aires, Editorial Planeta, 1996.

————. *Las zona oculta de tu signo.* Buenos Aires: Editorial Perfil, 1999.

————. *Las zonas erógenas de tu signo.* Buenos Aires: Editorial Perfil, 1998.

————. *El vampirismo.* Buenos Aires: Editorial Planeta, 1997.

————. *Cambia tu destino.* Buenos Aires: Editorial Perfil, 1997.

Jacobi, J. *La psicología de C. G. Jung.* Madrid: Espasa-Calpe, 1976.

————. *Formaciones de lo inconsciente.* Buenos Aires: Editorial Paidós, 1980.

Jung, Carl. *Memories, Dreams, Reflections.* New York: Editorial Jaffé, 1980.

Kaplan, S. *El sentido del sexo.* Barcelona; Editorial Grijalbo, 1981.

Keller, L. "Evolutionary Biology: All's Fair When Love Is War," *Nature* 373, no. 6511 (Jan. 19, 1995).

Launay, J. L., J. Levine, and G. Maurey. *El ensueño dirigido y el inconsciente.* Buenos Aires: Editorial Paidós, 1982.

Leuner, H. "The Role of Imagery in Psychotherapy." In *New Dimensions in Psychiatry: A Worldview,* edited by S. Arieti and Chrzanowski. New York: John Wiley, 1977.

McEwen, B. S. "Meeting Report: Is There a Neurobiology of Love?" *Molecular Psychiatry,* January 1997.

Meichenbaum, D. "Why Does Using Imagery in Psychotherapy Lead to Change?" In *The Power of Human Imagination,* edited by J. L. Singer and K. S. Pope. New York: Plenum, 1978.

Meishu, Sama. *El arte del Johrei.* Editorial Lux Orines.

Mokichi, Okada. *Luz de oriente.* Editorial Lux Orines. Atami, Japan 1967.

————. *Foundations of Paradise. Collected Writings.* Johrei Felloship.com, 1995.

Rosal, R. *El poder terapéutico de las imágenes.* Revista de psicoterapia, Barcelona, 1992.

Sarsby, Jacqueline. *Romantic Love and Society.* Middlesex: Penguin,1983.

Sheik, A. A. "Eidetic Psychotherapy." In *The Power of Human Imagination,* edited by J. L. Singer and K. Pope. New York: Plenum, 1978.

Shorr, J. E. *Psycho-Imagination Therapy: The Integration of Phenomenology and Imagination.* New York: Intercontinental Medical Book, 1972.

————. *Psychotherapy through Imagery.* New York: Intercontinental Medical Book, 1974.

Small, Meredith F. *What's Love Got to Do with It? The Evolution of Human Mating.* New York: Anchor Books, 1995.

Solot, Dorian, and Marshall Miller. *Unmarried to Each Other: The Essential Guide to Living Together as an Unmarried Couple.* New York: Marlowe & Company/Publishers Group West, 2002.

Velasco Suarez, C.A. *La actividad imaginativa en psicoterapia.* Buenos Aires, Editorial Universitaria, 1974.